STUPID CHRISTIANS

All Bible verses are from the NLT Bible unless otherwise stated.

Editor: Sharp Editorial

Cover design by Chantee The Designer & Co.

ISBN: 979-8-9863714-0-5 (paperback)

ISBN: 979-8-9863714-1-2 (hardback)

ISBN: 979-8-9863714-2-9 (eBook)

First printed edition published in 2023 in the United States of America

Paige Publishing

Orlando, Florida

STUPID CHRISTIANS

Why They Exist and How Not To Be One of Them

ERICA BERRY

PAIGE PUBLISHING

DEDICATION

I dedicate this book to my children – Paige, Roman, and Jackson. Don't be stupid. Read your Bible.

- Mom

TABLE OF CONTENTS

Dear Reader,

Let's discuss the elephant in the room – the title of this book. I know it's jarring, maybe a bit offensive, or a little bit of a trigger. I'm sure you're wondering who this book is for and why. Please allow me to explain myself. This book is for you. If the title piqued your interest enough for you to pick it up, then I believe God planned for this to happen. There's something within these pages you're supposed to see. To the believer, the new convert, and the veteran saint, this book is for you, but it isn't necessarily about you.

Let me explain.

By all accounts, I'd be considered a committed Christian. My entire life has been spent in church. I've led people to Jesus, preached sermons, led small groups, and played an active role in church leadership. You could say my life has been centered around God. There was only one problem—I didn't actually know Him. Several years ago, I realized that while I may have looked the part of a good Christian, the truth was that my relationship with God was superficial and shallow because I, like many Christians today, neglected one very important thing. I didn't prioritize God's Word. Don't get me wrong, I picked it up occasionally, but it was not a significant part of my Christian experience. Yes, you read that right. It's possible to be a "good Christian" without God.

You can sing, preach, and work for a God you don't know. We fail to realize that we can't possibly know God without reading His Word. God and His Word are one. It's a package deal. You can't love one without loving the other. But for a portion of my walk with Christ, I acted as if the Christian life is like Mattel and that God and the Bible were each sold separately. Sadly, if you've been around long enough, you can act the part well enough for your ignorance of Scripture, which tells us who God is, to be relatively undetected by others. I have found this to be the dangerous reality of most Christians.

I know how hypocritical this all sounds, but before you get "judgy" about my disclosure, I want to ask you how much of a priority has God's Word been in your life. Because statistics show that Bible reading is becoming increasingly less common for many believers. We live in an age of superficiality that has gone widely unchecked because our culture is consumed with image. We are encouraged to look like a Christian in public more than we are encouraged to act like one in private. This has led to a generation of stupid Christians who have no idea what they believe. And our ignorance is costing us big time! I stated that this book was for you but not about you. The consequences of your biblical ignorance are much more severe for the people you are called to evangelize. If you don't know the Word, you can't possibly share it with anyone else, and if you can't share it, how can they be saved?

When it comes to winning the lost to Christ, you are God's instrument of choice. You're it. You're all He has. So, your ignorance may not send you to hell, but it could certainly send your neighbor there. I know most Christian books don't take this kind of approach. I was warned not to be so antagonistic. I was told to tone it down a bit. Here's why I chose otherwise. I believe that God is using this book to sound the alarm on the dangers of spiritual apathy. I authored this book to challenge the status quo of Christianity and lovingly and confrontationally call believers to a higher standard.

I'm not all that concerned with whether you like or enjoy the book. This book was not written for your enjoyment; it was written to drag you out of the shallow end of the Christian experience and thrust you into the deep end of a passionate relationship with God and His Word. Friend, this book is a call to action. The goal is for this book to turn your comfortable little Christian life upside down.

Ready or not, here it comes.

CHAPTER ONE
Stupid Is a Choice

Stupid is a choice. There is no logical justification for ignorance in the 21st century, not with Google, Wikipedia, and YouTube, which offer information on any and every topic you can imagine. What you don't know is as readily available to you as the click of a button. If you don't know something today, it's likely because you don't want to know. You must choose ignorance. And this is where many believers find themselves in relation to knowing God and His Word.

Today's predominant problem for Christians has nothing to do with racial injustice or the attack on religious freedom. Our most significant issue does not stem from the effects of mental or physical illness or the highest rates of divorce and suicide in recent history. Today's greatest threat to Christianity is far less obvious but no less destructive. The problem is that most Christians are ignorant (better known as stupid, but I didn't want to start this book off on the wrong foot).

Ignorance is our greatest enemy because you can trace the origin of every one of the aforementioned issues to an ignorance of God and His Word. In case you don't believe me, here's proof. Hosea 4:6 says, *"My people are destroyed for lack of religious freedom? No. Lack of money? No. Lack of opportunity? No! My people are destroyed for lack of knowledge."* And the word *destroyed* is not code for something less catastrophic. It really means destroyed.

Simply put, a deficit in biblical knowledge opens the door to every type of deficit you could imagine. In this passage, God isn't talking to non-Christians. He's talking to His people. *His* people are destroyed just like those who don't know Him because ignorance leads to destruction.

What I noticed in my life wasn't just the occasional neglect of Bible reading, recitation, and study but a blatant disregard for Scripture. Imagine that—me, a good church-going, God-fearing Christian that never read her Bible.

Hard to imagine, right?

Unfortunately, I'm not alone.

A 2020 poll indicated that 34% of Christians said they never read their Bibles, and only 10% said they read their Bible four or more times a week.[1]

Ten percent!

So why don't well-meaning Christians read their Bibles? There are two main reasons. Firstly, it's because the devil is keenly aware of how powerful this book is in the hands of a believer. He knows that you can read your way out of poverty, marital discord, and even sickness when you apply the Word of God, so he works overtime to keep you distracted by life until

---

1 Statista. "Bible Readership in the U.S. 2018-2021." *Statista,* 22 July 2021, www.statista.com/statistics/299433/bible-readership-in-the-usa.

you're convinced that there is no room for Bible reading in your busy schedule. Secondly, it's because the Bible isn't given priority over other written works. It's seen as just another book. So when faced with problems in life, we esteem man's opinions over the authority of God. At the root of a lack of prioritization of the Word of God is an irreverence for God Himself. Western Christianity's idea of God as a homey, cool dude and BFF has crippled our ability to receive Him as Lord. A lack of reverence for God inevitably leads to devaluing His Word. I know I'm not alone when I state that it had become more normal for me to read books on healing than to read scriptures on healing. And if faced with an issue with my finances, I preferred Dave Ramsey's books, which are based on scriptural principles, over the actual scriptural principles themselves. For myself and many Christians just like me, sadly, Bible reading had become nothing more than an inconvenient optional activity, and I had the defeated life to prove it. The fact that I treated God's Word as an optional component of my Christian walk and then had the audacity to wonder why I wasn't growing spiritually or seeing success in my life proves my ignorance.

Now, when I speak of success, I'm not referring to ascending a corporate ladder or accumulating material things. Because I wasn't lacking in either of those areas. I'm talking about what the Scripture refers to as good success. Good success is the confidence that you are exactly where God wants you to be, doing the exact things He created you to do and possessing everything He wants you to have.

Most multi-millionaires don't have that kind of success, because there is nothing good about success without God.

——

Here's the thing—the rules have not changed. In Joshua 1:8, God tells His people how to be successful, and His recipe for success did not include positive affirmations, vision boards, networking, or higher education. His recipe for success was simple—it resulted from knowing God and His Word. And believe it or not, the same rules still apply.

"Study this Book of Instruction continually. Meditate on it day and night so you will be sure to obey everything written in it. Only then will you prosper and succeed in all you do."
(Joshua 1:8)

Sit with that Scripture for a moment. It's a shocker. Joshua 1:8 basically says that the journey to success begins with one thing: God's Word. That Scripture provides the blueprint for how your relationship with your Bible should look. Notice I said relationship. You can't have a relationship with an inanimate object, can you? The Word of God isn't merely a book. It's the living words of a living God. In Joshua 1, we're told that this book should consume our lives. When you think of being consumed with something, you think of the thing that keeps you up at night, wakes you up in the morning, and occupies your waking thoughts. It says to meditate on it day and night. I can't think of any time outside of day and night.

It's a bit jarring to think of God's standard for how much of a priority Scripture should be in our lives and how little of it we know or care to know. God isn't trying to be difficult when He asks us to prioritize His Word. He's doing this because He is His Word. He's basically inviting us into intimacy and fellowship with Him. And if you want a relationship with Him, you can't have it without a relationship with your Bible.

According to Joshua 1:8, this is how we are to relate to this book:

- Speak it
- Meditate on it
- Then do it

Only *then* you are promised good success in life. It's impossible to speak the Word without reading it. It's impossible to meditate on the Word without reading it. And it's certainly impossible to do the Word without reading it. So, let's put that Scripture in laymen's terms, shall we? The good life comes from good Bible reading, good Bible knowing, and good Bible living. And if this is true (and it is), may I ask to what or whom we attribute the success you've experienced in life? Because if the Word of God is not a part of your Christian experience, then your success may not be God-given.

Selah. (In other words, let that sink in.)

The problem with stupid Christians is not that they don't know the Word. The problem is they don't care that they don't know the Word.

———

The latter is far more of an indictment than the former. Most traditional religions place immense value on indoctrination, so much so that it happens at a very early age, and continued learning is introduced as a normal part of religious life, while Christians (at least the one writing this book) have been perfectly content being ignorant of the principles of their faith and are totally unaware of how dangerous it is to be this way. No other world religion tolerates this level of indifference from its believers. We fail to realize there is no greater enemy to the perpetuation of the Gospel than an ignorant Christian.

Why?

Because the problem isn't that stupid Christians don't reproduce themselves; it's that they do. We have created a culture in which it is entirely acceptable to be Christian in name only without the added burden of doing what a Christian is mandated to do. We have believed the lie that Christianity doesn't cost us anything and doesn't require any personal sacrifices. This kind of thinking has created an apathetic church in a perpetual state of powerlessness. Our lukewarm, modern Christianity goes out of its way to convince us that outside of a "sinner's prayer" and occasional church attendance, God requires nothing more from us. And that isn't true. Christians are *required* to grow in the knowledge of God. Unfortunately, we've become so accustomed to doing the bare minimum in our relationship with God that it does not phase us to be ignorant of His Word. I'd like you to consider the ridiculous notion of a non-Bible-reading Christian. It's like a lawyer who never studied law or a doctor who never studied medicine.

Sounds crazy, right?

Well, if that describes you, you are either a Christian who doesn't read the Bible (if you are, don't worry, you're not alone) or a new convert who doesn't yet know its importance; then this book was written just for you. I want you to see how crucial it is to prioritize a relationship with God's Word. Job realized its importance. He said he *"esteemed God's word more than his necessary food"* (Job 23:12).

Can you believe that?

Job said that the spiritual body could do without the Word of God no more than the human body could do without food. When you deprive the body of food, it can carry on as usual for a while and doesn't immediately break down. Eventually, however, your body will no longer supply the necessary nutrients to vital organs, and they will begin to shut down, leaving the body weak and unable to stave off death. Now, imagine your body as your spirit. If you don't feed your spirit with the Word of God, you may not notice any immediate effects. Eventually, however, your spirit will be as weak as a malnourished body, and you will render yourself defenseless against spiritual death.

Stupid Christianity produces unbelieving believers.

───

Stupid Christians are a group of people that identify themselves as believers but haven't a clue what to believe exactly. And I'm sure you aren't quite ready to admit that I'm describing you, so let me be honest and say I fit the description of an unbelieving believer at one point in my Christian life. Actually, I can pinpoint the exact moment when the repercussion of my stupidity smacked me in the face. And that moment led me on a journey of exploration of God and the Bible that completely changed my life. It was the catalyst for this very book. So, here's the story...

One day, I went to my mailbox, and to my surprise, there was an envelope with my home address on it, and the sender was listed as "Your Neighbor." Since the days of anthrax are long gone (if you weren't around in 2001, totally disregard that reference), I figured it wouldn't hurt to open it, so I did. I pulled out a handwritten two-page letter that began with "I know you don't know me, but...." Right then, I sensed this letter would be a doozy, so for sheer entertainment purposes, I decided to keep reading. The letter was from my neighbor, who identified herself as an affiliate of a particular religion, and for the retelling of this story, her religion will remain nameless. In the letter (which did I mention was two pages), she explained that she was concerned for my soul. She went on to detail her beliefs and why she believed what she believed, gave supporting arguments, and presented rebuttals for my hypothetical criticisms regarding her statements of "truth." To top it all off, she had the nerve to leave her name, phone number, and address so I could come to see her if I had any questions about what she wrote.

To me, those were fighting words.

I was utterly offended by the boldness with which she shared her faith. I was irritated by how intimidated she made me feel because I knew she could defend the falsehoods of her religious beliefs far more eloquently and thoughtfully than I could defend the truth of mine. I knew I could never take her up on her offer to see her because, with the knowledge she had about her faith and the ignorance I had concerning mine, she'd verbally chew me up and spit me out. What my neighbor did for me that day was provoke me in the best way. What my neighbor did that day was what birthed this book. Accepting that I had been backed into a proverbial corner was tough. It wasn't tough on my ego (although that also took a bit of a beating that day). It was tough on my conscience. What had happened was that I had the perfect setup, a divine opportunity, to share the truth of God's Word with my neighbor, and I missed it, not because I was unwilling or uncaring but because I was ignorant. And here's the part I may never get over—my ignorance did not cost me an argument; it cost me a soul.

I realized from that experience that it's not enough for me to feel momentary regret or disappointment. What separates a smart Christian from a stupid one is the deliberate actions to ensure that this scenario never happens again. So, suppose you're wondering why I'm so brash in my delivery about the severity of spiritual apathy and why I have the audacity to call anyone stupid. In that case, it's because I have been a stupid

Christian. I've been the Christian that prioritized reading books about how to have a better marriage, how to thrive in business, and how to be a great leader (all great topics that have no redemptive value) over reading the one Book that encompasses the keys to success in all those areas. I'm the stupid Christian who sat in church for years and let Scriptures be read to me like nursery rhymes but never read them for myself. I'm the stupid Christian who didn't realize that my relationship with the Word of God was equivalent to my relationship with God Himself because God is the Word. Whether we accept it, ignorance of the Word of God has dire consequences for us and those around us.

The best way to determine whether you know what you say you know is to test the degree to which you can defend what you know. When presented with the opportunity to share my faith, which is a non-negotiable Christian duty, I was unable to, not because I didn't love the Lord or hadn't been to church in a while, but because I didn't know enough about the Word to defend it. I can boldly defend that I am a woman. I don't just know it, but I am intimately acquainted with this fact every day. So, getting me to believe I'm anything other than a woman would be impossible. Thus, we must conclude that the missing element to your ability to share and defend the Word of God confidently is a lack of intimacy. There is no way you wouldn't defend your best friend if someone were to say something about them that wasn't true. You would have so much experience with them that it would be easy to negate a lie. However, if you were called upon to defend a stranger, you would be hard-pressed to come up with substantial evidence to support your claims because you don't know enough about them for your argument to bear any real weight. Let's admit it. Sadly, for most of us, God is nothing more than a stranger. We know as much about Him as we do any distant figure we admire.

So, how can you defend God?

You can only defend God when you know Him, and you can only know Him through fellowship in His Word.

> "In the beginning, the Word already existed. The
> Word was with God, and the Word was God."
> (John 1:1)

Famous biblical commentator Matthew Henry stated, "The Word had a being before the world had a beginning." How many times have you opened the Bible and treated it as if it were just another book, not realizing you were reading God's very own words? Friend, the only way to know God is by knowing His Word. It's much easier to be intimate with the Word when you approach it with the understanding that your relationship with it is your relationship with Him. I've often made this analogy: If my husband were to pass away, and the only thing I had that represented him was a handwritten letter he had addressed to me before he died, I'd cherish that letter. I'd likely read it repeatedly to the point of reciting it from memory. The words of that letter would be so ingrained in my mind because I'd realize that the closest thing I had to him would be what came directly from his heart. The Bible we hold in our hands is the handwritten letter we should cherish. It's our love note from God.

We must prioritize a relationship with the living Word of God because it is the only thing that has the power to change us and those around us. The goal of this book is to do for you what my neighbor's letter did for me.

I want to offend you.

I want to agitate you.

I want to provoke you to change.

We live in a very diplomatic, politically correct climate where we tiptoe around issues and walk on eggshells around each other to avoid offending. But what I've come to learn is that the avoidance of confrontation impedes positive change. Many people today are too sensitive. If you don't sprinkle a little sugar on your words, they can't seem to keep it down. I'm the opposite. If your offense provokes me to change, please, by all means, offend me.

I remember an intense argument with a close friend years ago. I felt she was hitting below the belt with her words in the argument. She began calling me out on some of my behaviors, and the more she did, the more upset I became. But looking back on that exchange, I can't recall her saying one thing that wasn't true. I realized she was confrontational because she cared about me, and she cared about us. And do you know what I did after that confrontation? I became agitated enough to change because she made me see that I needed it.

Well, I am willing to risk being confrontational with you because I care about you. So, when I use the term "stupid Christian," I'm doing so deliberately and thoughtfully. Do not be alarmed by my tone or writing style. It's just my way. But please know that it's coming from a place of love and, unfortunately, a place of panic. I'm concerned for this generation of believers. I'm concerned that we are not equipped to win the war that's coming, the spiritual battle we must fight to fulfill our assignment on Earth. The Bible instructs us to put on the whole armor of God. I don't know about you, but I don't see the need for armor if there is no fight. We are in a spiritual battle for our souls. Without armor, we are sure to get badly beaten in the process. So, I have made it my mission to convince believers to stop being willfully ignorant of the Word and pick up their Bible.

I'm a millennial, so I know how hard it can be to digest criticism. But I must warn you: If you are looking for a book or an author to butter your bread and act as if the stupid Christian label is meant to describe everyone but you, then put this book down now because this is not the book nor am I the author you're looking for. This book is a life raft. I'm throwing you a lifeline, a conscious interruption to your norm.

We can't afford to be stupid Christians any longer, especially in the condition of our world. Our world is in a pretty sad state. Now is the time for real Christians to take a stand to be the church and not just attend it. In fact, your church attendance often lulls you into a false sense of security that fosters willful ignorance. Westernized Christians will attend church to their detriment and are taught to depend on their pastor's knowledge and communication of Scripture. We fail to realize that an ignorant church is an impotent church.

Impotent: not potent; lacking in power, strength, and vigor; helpless.[2]

This definition sounds scarily similar to the current state of most Christians you know, doesn't it? When I was presented with the opportunity to share my faith with my neighbor but couldn't because I didn't know enough about my alleged beliefs, I was proving that ignorance leads to powerlessness.

I will make every effort to help you change the way you have viewed Scripture and to help you adopt a new, fresh way of relating to God's Word. I simply want you to fall in love with the Word of God. Fall in love with the God of the Word. We will take this journey together. So, if you can agree to forgive any offense you may incur from my delivery, I can agree to be nicer by the end of this book, and you will be so spiritually charged that you'll forget I called you stupid.

I toyed with calling this book In *Defense of the Faith, Do You Believe What You Believe*, or another catchier, non-threatening title. Ultimately, I decided to be authentic. My burden and calling are to introduce unbelievers to God and bring Christians closer to Him. How I do that may be unconventional, confrontational,

---

2 "Impotent." *Merriam-Webster.com*. 2022. https://www.merriam-webster.com (1 January 2021).

or aggressive, but I promise it will always be fueled by love. I'm not sure why you picked up a book with such a strange title or why I have been tasked with this uncomfortable assignment, but prayerfully, the intentions of this book are reached in the end, and that is to change unbelievers and challenge believers. The goal is to develop confrontational faith. That's what Jesus had. That's what my neighbor had. That's what you need.

If you're new to Christianity, this book is for you. If you've been a Christian for years, this book is for you. This book is a jumpstart to learning how to prioritize God's Word and will give you a better grasp of the biblical principles all Christians should live by and know. It's time to take your walk with the Lord to a new level.

If you're still reading, you have thicker skin than you realized and are ready to make some adjustments to the way you relate to God's Word. So, from one stupid Christian to another, let's go deeper. We've got some work to do.

CHAPTER TWO
ARE YOU "CHRISTIAN-ING" PROPERLY?

"Christian" isn't a label; it's a lifestyle. Here's the thing—many people consider themselves Christians but have no relationship with God.

How do I know this?

Because their attitude toward God's Word is their attitude toward God.

If you have zero relationship with His Word, knowing Him is impossible. It's equivalent to calling yourself a doctor because you want to be one or are passionate about helping people, but you've never seen a medical book. You, my friend, would not be a doctor; you'd be a very confused person, passionately confused, but confused, nonetheless. Life is meant to be built around God, not the other way around. For many, their lives are built around their ambitions, jobs, hopes, or dreams, and then they make time for God on weekends when convenient. For many Christians, if this were the year 2004, their relationship status with God on Facebook would be "it's complicated," unsure where you stand with each other.

Funny story—in my early 20s, I was once in a "relationship" with a guy who never called, never visited, and didn't claim me as his girlfriend. I posted our relationship status on Facebook as complicated, and a friend called to inquire about this guy. I told her about how indifferent he was toward me, and she finally broke the news that I was not, nor had I ever been, in a relationship with him. She didn't quite have the words to describe exactly what I had, so we mutually agreed that I didn't have anything at all.

I wonder what God would say about your relationship with Him. Would He say you never call, never visit, and don't claim Him in public? Friend, that's not Christianity. That's a "situation-ship." You claim Him when your situation calls for it. To be a true Christian, one must make God the center and everything else peripheral. There should be no questions about your commitment because it should be demonstrated in the seriousness you approach your relationship with Him.

One of the greatest barriers to knowing God and knowing and valuing His Word is our preoccupation with ourselves.

Let's face it—it's hard to be a Christian today. We don't exactly live in a society that encourages self-denial, but self-denial is one of the most critical components of authentic Christianity. Jesus said these words:

"Then he said to the crowd, 'If any of you wants to be my follower, you must give up your own way, take up your cross daily, and follow me.'"

(Luke 9:23)

We live in an age of extreme self-centeredness. Today, the vast majority of people are entirely self-absorbed and see absolutely no issues with it. Don't get me wrong—there have always been people who suffer from narcissism, but the difference is that what was once treated as a disorder has become a cultural norm. The Mayo Clinic defines a narcissistic personality type as having an inflated sense of self-importance.[3] The symptoms include:

- an excessive need for admiration
- disregard for others' feelings
- an inability to handle any criticism
- a sense of entitlement

If that doesn't describe most of the population, I don't know what does. The advent of social media has only exacerbated the normalization of self-centeredness. It's created a culture where you can be as braggadocious, obnoxious, and self-promoting as you want. The only difference is now you can call it "branding." Think about it—we live in a world where everyone has their own website, a public display of their awesomeness, and a shrine of themselves that they update daily. This has encouraged us to be more preoccupied with how we look than with who we are inside. Quite frankly, we have grown entirely and utterly distracted with ourselves.

---

3 "Narcissistic Personality Disorder - Symptoms and Causes." *Mayo Clinic*, 18 Nov. 2017, www.mayoclinic.org/diseases-conditions/narcissistic-personality-disorder/symptoms-causes/syc-20366662.

Enter another post-modern concept that people love: Cropping. Cropping allows you to take out whatever you don't like. Once it's cropped, it's as if it never existed. Don't we all know a little bit about that? Whether Christians know it or not, they avoid reading Scripture because they can't handle the truth, not biblical truth but personal truth. James 1:23 provides a vivid analogy about how the Bible affects us. He says that when we read the Bible, it's as if a man is looking at himself in a mirror. The Bible shows you who you really are as you read it and measure your life up to its standard. We tend not to like the flaws we see when we look into the mirror of God's Word. It's become much easier when confronted with the bad parts of our humanity instead of fixing them or facing them, cutting them out as if they aren't there.

And to further complicate matters, enter Christianity.

Here's the hard truth: It's tough to be a humble, self-denying, culture-challenging, God-fearing Christian today. In fact, the non-conformists willing to die to themselves and live for God at the expense of acceptance and popularity in an age when everyone seems to be clamoring for more likes and views are made to seem weird and out of touch.

You also can't have the love and admiration of this world *and* the approval of the Father. If nothing about your life clashes with the culture of the world, it's most likely because they have too much in common. My friend, in order to Christian properly, you must choose.

Sorry to burst your bubble, but Christianity is a life of

But the bottom line is that you can't serve God and yourself at the same time.

—

sacrifice. You are not signing up for a cakewalk. If you want a life of ease, please choose something else because this isn't it. And I'd hate for you to get to the end of your life and face God in shame because you believed the lie that your life was about you. This may be surprising, but here is the cold hard truth: There is no gray with God. It's either His way or no way, and the way is narrow. Jesus said so in Matthew 7:13-14:

You can enter God's Kingdom only through the narrow gate. The highway to hell is broad, and its gate is wide for the many who choose that way. But the gateway to life is very narrow and the road is difficult, and only a few ever find it.

I understand it's a hard pill to swallow that you're not the main character in your story, but your life is about Him, including the business you run, the talents you possess, the city you live in, and the person you marry. When you add it all up, it equals His Will. It's His story. He is the star in this life, and you are a supporting role. You are a created being. You were created for the glory of God. The creation is never greater than the creator, and no creator creates something to do the opposite of what He designed it to do.

"Bring all who claim me as their God, for I have made them for my glory. It was I who created them."

(Isaiah 43:7)

If your life looks more like it's for your glory, I must humbly insist you are not Christian-ing properly at all. When God is central to your life's story, He writes and directs the script of your life. You're just an actor on His main stage of humanity. You exist to act out His Will, and if you do it well, it will make people want to stand and applaud the Creator of the story more than they applaud the one playing the role. Being a true Christian means that God is the goal, the pursuit, and the reward. The best way to identify if you're Christian-ing properly is to identify who is at the center of your story. And it's not enough for you to insist that it's God without concrete evidence to prove it.

I've got good news and bad news. I'll give you the good news first: Reorganizing your life around God is simple, but the bad news is that it isn't easy. This world is filled with distractions, things pulling for your heart and your time, but

The secret to a successful relationship with God always begins with descending the throne of your life and letting God occupy the throne in your place.

—

God does not require you to make Him your only priority, but you must make Him your first priority. If you are ready to prioritize your walk with the Lord, you must start with the thing that brings you closest to Him: His Word.

CHAPTER THREE
Have You Read the Directions?

You may be wondering what's the big deal with the Bible. Do we actually need to read it to be a Christian? The answer to this question is an emphatic yes, and here's why—When seeking to operate anything, the first rule of thumb is to read the directions.

I'm the builder in my house. My husband is a fantastic businessman, golfer, and dad, but builder he is not. He has the potential to be a great builder, but I don't think he'll ever be one because he lacks one essential quality—he has an aversion to directions. Like most men, he looks at the parts and believes he's smart enough to build the object without consulting the instructions of the person who created the thing. He recently put together a desk for my daughter's room (I use the term "put together" very loosely). It was a simple desk, nothing special, with four legs and one small drawer. My dear husband took a few glances at the picture on the box and figured he could freestyle the build. He took out all of the parts of the desk, set aside the hardware, and went for it. At first glance, the desk looked perfect. My daughter was happy to come home from school to find her brand-new desk. She used it every day for about a month, but one day, one of the legs buckled, and the desk started to lean. The following day, she couldn't open the drawer without it coming off the track. Shortly after that, her cute little desk was in a cute little heap of broken parts in our garage. As my husband and I stood there looking at the fragments of the desk, I thought it was a good time to ask him this question- "Honey, did you read the directions?" Needless to say, that inquiry was too little too late.

My daughter's desk reminds me of many Christians I know. We expect to build and manage life without consulting the Directions of the One who created us. Sure, everything appears fine for a while, but eventually, the cracks begin to show, and before we know it, we've got a mess of a life because we failed to do one really important thing—read the Directions.

The Bible is a manual for life. Someone once coined this acronym for the Bible:

B - Basic

I - Instructions

B - Before

L - Leaving

E - Earth

The Word of God provides the instructions we need for living a victorious life. If you don't want victory, then by all means, don't read the Bible. But if you're going to operate this life to its optimum capacity, from your marriage to your business, there's only one way to do it: habitually reading God's Word.

Let me be clear. Reading the Bible does not change you. Many Bible scholars and theologians are well acquainted with

Scripture but strangers to its power, and here's why.

The Word of God isn't just text on a page. It's a living document with power.

Why does it need power, you ask?

Because the Word of God actually works on your heart. It cleanses, sanctifies, heals, and gives you the power to overcome our common enemy, the devil, whose only job is to kill, steal, and destroy us for good. In Ephesians 6, the Word of God is referred to as a sword. It defends you from the devil's antics and enables you to guard yourself against his many attacks.

The Bible doesn't change us. It tells us the reasons why we need to change.

—

I love how the apostle Paul describes how the Word works in the life of believers. In Hebrews 4:12, he describes the Word of God using four attributes. According to Paul, your Bible is

1. Living
2. Powerful
3. Sharp
4. Discerning

Do those words describe an inanimate object?

No. Those words describe a living document. Let's break down those attributes, one by one, so you get the whole picture.

The Word is *living*.

The KJV of Hebrews 4:12 says that the Word is "quick and powerful." The Greek translation of the word *quick* in this passage means not just alive but lively. Some translations describe the word as active. Let's understand why the Word is considered active. The Word of God is active because it's got work to do. It convicts us of our sins and grabs our attention by cutting away the maladies of the spirit. Then, it comforts us and stitches up the wounds from that cut to mold us into the image of Christ we were created to be. Sounds pretty active to me.

The Word is *powerful*.

The power of God is experienced and revealed through His Word. Perhaps there is no greater demonstration of the Word's power than when we see what it does to a soul that was once dead to sin. No other written work by any other author in history has the power to bring dead things to life. II Timothy 3:15 says, "the Holy Scriptures are able to make you wise for salvation through faith which is in Christ Jesus." This simply means that the Word of God, when mixed with our faith, has the power to mark a clear path to eternal life. Name another book with that much capacity. I'll wait...

The Word is *sharp*.

The Word of God has laser precision, able to precisely cut away the sinful nature that has become so ingrained in our souls. According to Hebrews 4:12, it is said to pierce even to the division of soul and spirit and joints and marrow, which simply means the Word of God is sharp enough to divide the most intricately connected parts of you. It's tough to decipher where the bone ends and marrow begins. That's how close they are together. So it is with our sins. Sin can become such a part of our souls that it may be hard to make a precise dissection. But the Word is as sharp as a sword and can do the exact work in you that your condition calls for.

The Word is *discerning*.

The Word of God discovers and uncovers your true condition. You can't measure the state of something without having a model for how it should look. The Word is our model. It reveals where you are compared to where you should be and makes it impossible to hide from the truth. Simply put, you don't read the Bible; the Bible reads you. James 1:23 refers to the Word of God as a mirror. If you want to know what you really look like, read your Bible and compare your image to the image God intends for you to have.

Let's look at some additional ways the Word works in our lives.

The Word is a **weapon**.

In Ephesians 6:17, the Word of God is described as the "sword of the spirit." I don't know many people who walk around with a sword. You only need a sword if you need a weapon. As Christians, we are in a daily fight for our souls. We are given the Word of God because if we are ever going to have a fighting chance at succeeding in our spiritual battle, we will need to arm ourselves. And our weapons can't be natural ones. They must be spiritual because our enemy is a spirit.

The Word is **medicine**.

You may be less familiar with this, but the Word of God can heal your physical body as much as it can heal your soul.

"My child, pay attention to what I say. Listen carefully

to my words. Don't lose sight of them. Let them
penetrate deep into your heart, for they bring life
to those who find them, and healing to their whole
body."
(Proverbs 4:20-22)

"He sent out his word and healed them, snatching
them from the door of death."
(Psalm 107:20)

God's Word brings healing to the spirit, mind, and body of the Christian.

Can you believe that?

Studying the Word can produce physical healing. There was once a great man of God named Derek Prince, who happens to be one of my all-time favorite Bible teachers. Derek Prince tells of a time when he was injured in the army. He was in the infirmary for months but not improving. In fact, his condition worsened, as there was no cure for his illness. As he lay in his hospital bed, he picked up his Bible and stumbled across Psalm 107:20. When he read it, a light bulb went off, and he realized that the Word of God was medicine. He then reasoned that if the Word was medicine, he should start taking the Word as he took his prescribed medication—three times a day with food. So, a nurse would administer his pain medication during every meal, and when the nurse administered his natural medication, he would open his Bible and administer his spiritual medication. Slowly but surely, he experienced total healing in his body of an incurable disease that his doctors were simply managing. His natural medicine was merely helping him endure the illness, but the Word of God healed him completely.

We started this book by discussing the dangers of neglecting the Word of God. Well, your Bible is like a pill with the potential to heal your physical disease, but instead of taking the pill, you leave the bottle unopened by your bedside as your health slowly deteriorates. You would be crazy not to take that pill. If you leave your Bible unopened, you forfeit your right to spiritual, physical, and emotional healing.

The Word is **therapy**.

You've learned about the Word's ability to heal spiritually and physically, but I recently witnessed the Word's power to heal emotionally. One of my dear mentees recently lost her 21-month-old son in a tragic accident when his caregiver left him in a hot car for hours. I've seen mothers deal with the loss of a child but never had I seen a woman so broken as my mentee regarding the passing of her sweet baby boy. I watched as she battled depression and suicidal thoughts. She was wasting away, refusing to eat, and became a lifeless shell of a woman.

One day, I saw her in church and noticed she was struggling. So, I pulled her into a side room. I struggled to find the words to comfort her as she wept in my arms. What is there to say to someone in that much pain? As her heart was breaking, I looked her in the eyes and said, "The only thing that will get you through this is the Word." I was almost alarmed at the words as they exited my mouth. I sincerely hoped she didn't feel like I was trivializing her pain or seeking to put a temporary bandage on an extremely painful permanent situation. But those words came from the depths of my heart. I was offering the only thing I knew would save the life of a woman on the brink. I told her I needed her to get to know the God of the Bible, who is close to the brokenhearted. So, I gave her a book to get her started, and she took off on a quest to learn more about God through His Word.

Weeks of Bible study turned into months, and slowly but surely, I watched as she allowed the Word to heal her heart and breathe life back into her physical body. I had never witnessed anything like it. The Word of God has the power to search for your greatest need and heal you completely, physically, spiritually, and emotionally.

I don't know what you may be facing, but I know that the key to success in any area is found within the pages of your Bible. You can't possibly manage life on your own. And if you're looking for a solution, no matter the problem, the answer is simple. All you need to do is read the Directions.

CHAPTER FOUR
Unbelieving Believers

If I were to ask the average church-going Christian if they were a believer, I assume the answer would likely be yes. However, there are two issues with that exchange:

1. The question
2. The response

Neither are comprehensive enough to ascertain anything substantial about their relationship with God. One of the church's fundamental problems is the prevalence of "unbelieving believers." In my experience, my problem, which could also be your problem, is that I said I was a believer but couldn't articulate what I believed.

More than ever, we live in a time when more Christians don't go to church or read their Bibles, causing our standards for a true follower of Jesus Christ to be increasingly compromised to

Today, we slap the Christian label on people who haven't proven it applies to them.

—

accommodate the lukewarm masses. Actually, the best place to find a stupid Christian is the church. They attend church without the added burden of doing what is required to know God for themselves.

My friend, regardless of whether you choose to live up to the standards of Christianity, they have not and will never change. So, instead of wanting to do the bare minimum for being a Christ-follower and trying to redefine and lower the standards of believers, why don't you meet the requirements and part ways with stupid Christianity once and for all? If you call yourself a believer, let's make sure you qualify that claim with demonstrable knowledge. In this chapter, my goal is to help you understand the basics of precisely what believers believe.

Faith and Belief

Your faith is *nothing* without belief. Your conviction, which is often rooted in emotion, can be easily dismantled when challenged if it does not have concrete beliefs to back it up. That is why it is so dangerous to be an unbelieving believer because when your faith is tested, you won't have enough knowledge not to be shaken.

Have you ever encountered a person who said they believed God to be a healer, but then God didn't heal a loved one, and it caused them to lose faith in God's ability? This is the exact consequence of being an unbelieving believer.

Your belief is your foundation. Our greatest defense against

True belief in God's Word keeps you standing even when disappointed.

the adversaries of our faith is knowing what and in whom we believe. So, when I ask you what you believe, if the answer isn't wrapped tightly in Scripture, what may feel like faith may be an emotional response to rhetoric. And we all know how reliable emotions are, right (insert sarcasm)?

Hindrances to Faith

One would assume that the greatest threats to faith are suffering, persecution, and great trials, but those aren't enough to dismantle faith. If you truly know what you believe, your trials only strengthen your faith because they prove that our God is the only One to sustain us amid our hardships. The greatest hindrance to your faith is something less obvious. It's called deception. Deception is when something fake looks and sounds so much like the real thing that it's difficult to distinguish between them. Not knowing what you believe makes you a prime candidate for deception. This is the danger of being an unbelieving believer. Ignorance and deception go hand in hand.

As for the question, "what do Christians believe," I find many Christians aren't quite sure. And because they aren't sure, they are easily deceived.

So, what is the solution?

Don't fight unbelief with belief. Fight unbelief with the truth. So, here's the truth...

Five Core Beliefs of the Christian Faith

Every Christian must subscribe to these five core beliefs to qualify as a believer. Without an agreement with these core tenants, there is no basis for your faith.

1. Only one God exists eternally as Father, Son, and Holy Ghost.

    •   God the Father is God, God the Son is God, and God the Holy Spirit is God. There are not three separate Gods. There is one God who has always existed at the same time as Father, Son, and Holy Spirit but with specific and distinct roles. What you believe about God is important because what you believe about Him determines how you treat Him. Suppose God is a mythical being that you've never accepted as real. In that case, your relationship with Him will be distant, and He will always feel out of reach to you spiritually and emotionally. If God is real to you, your connection to Him will be personal, and you will reap the benefits of intimacy with Him.

2. Jesus is the only way to God (salvation).

    •   There aren't many ways to God. You can't get to God through any other means than through belief in and acceptance of the way of salvation which is Jesus Christ. Salvation cannot be earned; it must be received. We are saved by faith in Jesus Christ alone. Jesus' death, burial, and resurrection solved the separation issue between God and man caused by sin. That is what we mean when we say that Jesus is the way to God. Through His blood, we are no longer separated from our Heavenly Father. (More on this in the section *The Real Jesus*.)

3. The resurrection of Jesus Christ.

•   Belief in the death, burial, and resurrection of Jesus is a foundational truth of the Christian faith. In fact, the totality of our faith hangs on this one fact—Jesus Christ died and was raised back to life. I challenge you to ascertain whether the resurrection of Jesus in your mind and heart is a fairytale or as real to you as your very existence. We must believe that Jesus died and rose again because we can't be saved without this belief. This is why Jesus refers to Himself as the door in John 10:9: *"I am the door; by me, if any man enter in, he shall be saved..."*. We come into covenant and communion with God through faith in the work of His Son.

4. Jesus was both God and man.

•   Jesus Christ is God wrapped in human flesh. Jesus did not stop being God when He came to Earth. It was no more possible for Him to lay His deity aside than for us to lay our humanness aside. Jesus was God the whole time because Jesus is God all the time.

5. The Bible is the final authority on all matters and is error-proof.

• If Scripture is God-breathed (and it is), it is without error and can be trusted completely because God cannot lie. God's Word originated in Heaven, and men were the channels through which the Word was given, but God is the source because He is the one who inspired men to write what is recorded in Scripture.

Are you ready for your first challenge?

Okay, here it is.

Take each of those five beliefs and find two Scriptures to support each. Write down your supporting Scriptures beside the core belief for your reference. It's not enough for you to read about the core beliefs without becoming acquainted with them. The best way to do this is to open your Bible and discover why these beliefs are true.

And go!

No, really, stop reading and grab your Bible. I will be waiting for you when you return.

The Gospel

If I were to ask you what the Gospel is, you'd likely be familiar enough with that word to give me the definition you've heard in church at some point. The Gospel is "Good News." Indeed, the Gospel is Good News, but here's likely where we would part ways in agreement. Most of us believe that the good news is that Jesus saves. He came to Earth, was born of a virgin, died, and took the penalty of our sins on the cross so that we would be made right with God. Our sins have been forgiven, and we have eternal life when we accept and believe what Jesus did. This explanation, while true, is incomplete. The Gospel message isn't that Jesus saves. The fact that Jesus saves is good news, but it isn't *the* Good News. The Gospel message spoken of in Scripture is more than salvation. It's about the Kingdom of God. Salvation is included in the Gospel but isn't the central theme.

Before you check out completely, let me explain. The phrase most often used in Jesus' teachings about the Gospel is not just the Gospel but the Gospel of the Kingdom. We don't get the full scope of the Gospel if we leave out the concept of the Kingdom of God. If you look up the word Gospel every time it appears in Scripture, it is most often accompanied by the word Kingdom. One of the best examples of this (there are many) is Jesus' own words: *"'The time promised by God has come at last!' he announced. 'The Kingdom of God is near! Repent of your sins and believe the Good News!'"* (Mark 1:15).

This passage makes it clear that the Kingdom of God is central to the Gospel message because the Gospel is the Good News. "What exactly is that Good News" is the next logical question. Well, before I answer that question, I need to bring some understanding to what is meant by the "Kingdom of God."

The Kingdom of God is better understood as the government of God. That concept may be hard to understand because of our limited experience with that kind of governance. We live in a democratic society governed by elected representatives put in place by the people's votes. These representatives form a collective that rules the land. This is what we understand to be democratic rulership. Kingdoms are not democracies. They are better explained as monarchies. A monarchy is a country ruled by a monarch or one central head of state. The Kingdom of God is best understood in this way. God is the head of a nation of people under His complete sovereignty and rule. Simply put, the Kingdom of God is the government of God. It's a life where God is the One in charge.

Now let's put it all together. If the Kingdom were a physical building, Jesus would be the door. There would be no access to the building unless you passed through the door. Jesus, through His sacrifice and our acceptance of it, gives us access to the Kingdom of God, where God dwells and rules. The good news is that we will once again (and once and for all) come under the government of God. God will once again take over the government of the human race. In the beginning, Adam and Eve enjoyed life under God's rule, and that's why their lives were idyllic. Creation wasn't about God fulfilling the urge to make stuff. It was God, as King, establishing His Kingdom on Earth. One day, this Earth will again be ruled by a government whose head is God, not politicians. That is the Gospel. In this context, salvation is understood not to be an escape from this world but the restoration of a world as it was originally designed.

The Real Jesus

Who is Jesus?

No, not the one you imagined when I said his name. I mean, who is the real Jesus?

This question is the most important question you will ever answer because your understanding or lack thereof of the person and work of Jesus Christ is the foundation upon which your salvation rests. Your salvation is your access to the Kingdom of God. The easiest way for the enemy to keep you from the gift of salvation is for him to keep Jesus as a mystery to you. That's not to say that you will understand everything there is to know about Him, but you can know Him more deeply and truly through His Word. You may think you already know who He is, but I'd like to focus on a particular aspect that helps shed more light on His nature.

The aspect of Him we will deal with now is His righteousness. I want to begin the discussion of who people understand Jesus to be by finding out what they think it means to be good. If I were to ask you what it means to be righteous, you might formulate a mental list of all the things that qualify you for this label. You are honest and kind, you go to church, you pray, and so forth. But what if I told you those things were the exact opposite of what it means to be righteous? If you don't immediately think of Jesus when defining righteousness, you don't understand Him.

Every aspect of Jesus' earthly life pointed to the fact that He was not just a man; He was the Word of God wrapped in human flesh. He was righteous because He was righteousness. He did not sin because there was no sin in Him. He was God in the flesh. If you don't first understand that the definition of righteousness is Jesus, you are not ready to accept the work that His blood did for us on the cross. When man fell and became plagued with the disease of sin, the only thing that could right our wrongs was a perfect sacrifice. The cross was not just an act of love but an act of justice because our Holy God simply could not forgive the sins of mankind without them being paid for first. The Bible says in Romans 6:23 that the wages (payment) of sin is death. Wherever there is sin, something has to die because death is the direct consequence of sin. And the only way to fix the impending death of mankind was to have something or someone else die in its place. Those wages had to be paid one way or another. Think of it this way—if you had to go before the judge in court because of a stack of speeding tickets you incurred due to reckless driving, you would be held accountable for those violations, and the penalty would be a huge fine or jail time. Let's say you couldn't pay the fine, but someone approached the judge and offered to pay your fines. The judge would have to declare you legally innocent because the debt would have been paid in full. That's like what Jesus did for us. There was no way we could pay the fine for our sins, so Jesus stepped up and paid it for us with His life, and God the Father declared our innocence. Jesus died the death that we deserved.

But why Jesus?

Jesus was the only person qualified to be the sacrifice (death payment) for our sins because He was the only righteous person. He was God in the flesh, so He was the only man in history who experienced the temptations of life and did not yield. When He died, there was a trade. He said to mankind that He would trade your sin for His righteousness. On the cross, He put on sin so that we could put on righteousness.

Have you ever switched clothes with a sibling or a friend? That's kind of what took place through Jesus' death on the cross. We exchanged the garment of sin for the garment of righteousness. He took the penalty our sin deserved, and we now enjoy the reward His righteousness affords. So, in this instance, being a good person has nothing to do with your righteousness. In fact, when it comes to receiving salvation, the worst thing you can be is a "good person."

Too often, people's estimation of their goodness keeps them from realizing their need for His righteousness.

—

If I see myself as good, it makes the cross seem unnecessary to me. That's why the Bible never asks us to be good; it instructs us to be holy. Goodness and righteousness are completely different. Goodness is earned, but righteousness is received, not earned. It isn't a title; it's attire. We are clothed in righteousness when we have faith in the finished work of Jesus. This is why Isaiah 64:6 says that our righteous deeds are like filthy rags. Our goodness is so far removed from Christ's righteousness that His righteousness makes our goodness look like filth. We are made righteous by faith, not by doing good because doing good to prove our righteousness is an insult to the work of the cross.

Why did He do all of this?

He did this so you and I could be reconciled (brought back) to God.

Before sin, God's design for mankind was that He would dwell among His creation without separation. After sin, there was a veil between God and man. Jesus came so that the veil would be torn and mankind's relationship with God would be restored.

So, who is Jesus?

Jesus is indeed who He says He is: The way, the truth, and the life. And no one comes to the Father except through Him.

What Does It Mean To Be Saved?

The answer to this question is found in blood.

Let me explain.

You can't truly understand salvation until you understand

atonement. Atonement was a significant theme in the Old Testament, but it suddenly disappeared in the New Testament, and here's why. Atonement is better understood by the term "reconcilement." Simply put, it's how a broken relationship is made right. Remember that God's space and man's space were one and the same in the beginning. There was no separation between God and His creation. God was pleased to dwell with Adam and Eve in a real and consistent way, as depicted by the fellowship they enjoyed in the Garden of Eden. However, man's sin broke our relationship (fellowship) with God. When Adam and Eve sinned, the immediate punishment was not death but separation from God. They were no longer able to share space with their Creator. But Jesus' blood fixed the broken relationship between God and man. Let me tell you how.

The History of Atonement

Each time a person sinned in the Old Testament, God demanded a blood sacrifice for that sin to be forgiven.

Whenever there is sin, something has to die because the payment for sin is death.

—

"In fact, according to the law of Moses, nearly
everything was purified with blood. For without the
shedding of blood, there is no forgiveness."
(Hebrews 9:22)

Before Jesus' death on the cross, God accepted the blood sacrifice of animals as atonement for man's sin. But it couldn't just be any animal. It had to be an animal without a blemish or spot. It had to be the perfect specimen of the animal.

Why?

Because a sacrifice isn't a real sacrifice unless it hurts.

Back then, people loved their animals. Animals represented a means of survival and contributed to wealth. So, if someone wanted to make a blood sacrifice to request forgiveness for their sins, they wouldn't take one of the defective animals they could stand to lose. They were required to take the best of the flock because the act of sacrifice does not work unless you offer something you love. When the blood of that animal was shed, that sacrifice would suffice to make things right with God, and that blood would cover that sin.

Christ's Atonement

What God wants most is fellowship with you and me, but sin breaks that fellowship with God. So, God devised a plan to reconcile, to restore the broken relationship between Himself and man, by offering a blood sacrifice once and for all. But it wasn't just any sacrifice. It was a perfect sacrifice. He gave His one and only son, Jesus (the perfect lamb), as payment for the sins of mankind. Jesus' blood atoned for the sins of the world and restored the fellowship between God and man. That's why blood sacrifice disappears in the New Testament as a means of atonement. Jesus Christ was the last and final sacrifice. That's salvation! Salvation is accepting the finished work of Jesus' blood on the cross and taking advantage of the restored access to God that His blood affords.

CHAPTER FIVE
It's Just a Story

Raise your hand if you've ever been intimidated by the thought of reading the entire Bible.

I've felt the same way.

I want to relieve you of your apprehension about reading God's Word. And the best way to do so is to provide a basic yet comprehensive summary of the Bible. I want you to see that the Bible is just a story. Once you understand its premise, everything in between makes much more sense.

I'd venture to say more of us would read our Bibles consistently if we understood the storyline. My interest in Scripture grew when I developed a basic understanding of the point of this book. I'm no theologian, but that's okay. I think it's perfectly fine to approach the Scriptures as someone who may not always understand everything but is committed to growing in their understanding. We may not all be Bible scholars, but we should be Bible students at the very least. Here's a disclaimer: I am just a student. I don't know all there is to know about the Word, but I'm in a committed relationship with the God of the Word, and He and His Word are a package deal. So, let's get a basic understanding of the story of the Bible so that it becomes more relatable. And don't worry—I'm not smart enough to confuse you, so you won't have any problems understanding this summary. Who knew being a stupid Christian had benefits?

A Collection of Books

The Bible is a collection of books. Among them are history books, law books, and poetry books, but they correlate with helping you form an understanding of God. The word Bible is plural. It comes from the Latin word *Biblia* which means books. So, the Bible can be better understood as a library of books. When you attended school, you had multiple subjects intended to work together to build a basic foundation for knowledge. In your school library, there were history books, math books, science books, etc., but you learned these topics simultaneously to gain the knowledge needed to frame your understanding of the world. The Bible can also be understood in this way. The Bible contains a collection of books written by about 40 different authors at different times, but the purpose of this collection is to frame your understanding of God. More than being a collection or library of books, the Bible can also be understood as one big story, but it isn't just any story. The Bible is the history of the entire world. It is a story of a King and His Kingdom. And with this basic foundation, let's begin.

Old Testament

As with any book, you likely won't be invested in the story if you don't understand the point. So, here's the plot: God wants to build a kingdom on Earth, among the people He created, to last forever, and **nothing** will stop His plan.

The Bible provides an undeniably reliable historical account of our world. In addition to being a book of history, the Bible is a book of prophecy as it sometimes foretells centuries in advance of historical events that have been documented and indisputably certified.

Let's build your understanding of the Bible as the story of the world and why you must understand it to understand the Gospel.

In the Beginning

The book of Genesis provides the account of the beginning of mankind. God, who has always existed, created everything. He made the Heavens and the Earth. The entire world is the result of His creative mastery. I've always been amused at how the Bible does nothing to explain the origin of God. Many atheists are obsessed with answering the question, "where did God come from?" The Bible simply begins with God to prove that it's a ridiculous notion to question whether He exists. Clearly, only an entity greater than us could have created us. Only a being outside of time and matter could have created time and matter. It isn't rocket science.

This supreme being created all that we see. And why did He

create the world?

The short answer is He created the world for His glory. Any creation bears proof of the existence and creativity of its creator. Quite simply, the world was created to be the proof of God. This is better explained by the fact that God created man in His image: *"So God created human beings in his own image. In the image of God, he created him; male and female he created them"* (Genesis 1:27).

An image is better understood as a copy. It points to the original or *glorifies* the original.

The setting of the story of the beginning of man is a place called Eden. God created a paradise and set man in the middle of it. In this paradise, God's space and man's space were one and the same. Nothing was separating God from man, and God wanted it that way. He wanted to live among His creation, ruling and leading them within the new kingdom He was established on Earth. He was the King, ruling His Kingdom, and had an intimate relationship with His subjects.

God was good to Adam and Eve, and they had everything they needed in this beautiful place, but there was one caveat, a warning: Do not eat of the tree of the knowledge of good and evil. Sadly, Adam and Eve disobeyed God's command, and sin entered the world. Immediately, everything changed. Because of their disobedience, the man and woman were banished from their paradise and sentenced to a life of toil, becoming responsible for cultivating by hard labor what had originally been a byproduct of citizenship in God's Kingdom. But the toil wasn't the punishment. The punishment was separation from God.

Because God is holy, He hates sin. The minute sin entered Eden, it separated God and mankind. The original plan for a kingdom where the King and His people lived together was temporarily undermined.

Here is an excellent place to introduce a theme seen throughout Scripture: The concept of redemption. No plan of God goes undone, and no matter what happens to undermine God's Will, He never gives up. He eventually finds a way to redeem His original plan.

As more men and women populate the Earth, sin spreads like a plague. There is a telling Scripture in Genesis 6 that tells us the condition of the world at that time: *"The Lord observed the extent of human wickedness on the earth, and he saw that everything they thought or imagined was consistently and totally evil"* (Genesis 6:5).

The effects of sin had damaged creation, and God only had one choice: to rid the world of evil by wiping out the entire human race with a flood, starting with a new race of people to usher righteousness back into the world. God does just that with a righteous man named Noah, whom God chose to restart His redemptive plan for humanity (Genesis 6:5-8). Noah became something like a "new Adam" as he and his family were kept safe in the flood that wiped out everything and everybody else, and his descendants became the founding fathers of a brand-new population. Noah's three sons were Japheth, Shem, and

Ham, and they populated various parts of the world and are responsible for the different races of people we now have. After the flood, God established a covenant with Noah as His representative for all mankind. He made a covenant with Noah that He would never again destroy the Earth with water.

Covenant: a formal and serious agreement or promise.[4]

Here is something interesting to note when God makes a covenant: No matter what circumstances arise to thwart that promise, God never abandons His end of the deal. We will see this theme played out in Scripture repeatedly.

Unfortunately, as Noah's sons re-populate the Earth, the effects of sin begin to rear their ugly heads again, and once more, sin causes a breakdown of the relationship between God and man. It all reaches a climax with the building of the Tower of Babel (a tower meant to go to Heaven), which was nothing more than an act of rebellion toward God as men chose their own will over God's Will. At the beginning of Genesis, God told man to fill the Earth to expand the Kingdom of God, and He never took away that mandate. However, the Tower of Babel was man's attempt to make a name for themselves in one place so that they wouldn't be scattered all over the Earth and would maintain control. God ensures that His plan succeeds, despite man's rebellion, and He halts the building of this tower by confusing the languages of

---

4 "Covenant." Merriam-Webster.com. 2022. https://www.merriam-webster.com (1 January 2021).

man. The ensuing chaos causes them to separate and spread, just as God had originally intended. God always gets His way!

The next main character (and one of the most critical figures in biblical history) is Abraham, a descendant of Shem. After the disaster of the Tower of Babel, God once again sets in motion a plan of redemption and chooses one man to birth a new breed of people to usher righteousness back into the land. (Do you see the redemptive pattern?) The lineage of Abraham is what we call the Jews/Israelites. God handpicked Abraham to father a chosen nation of people. These people would represent God's redemptive plan for humanity. Amid a world full of sin and evil, they would love, honor, and serve the Lord and be the beneficiaries of His blessing. Do you remember the beginning of this story when I explained Eden as a place under God's complete rule and Adam and Eve reside within this paradise governed by God? Well, the Israelites were handpicked to be the people through whom God would reinstate His rulership on Earth, and to do so, God would give them a special Promised Land (their own kind of Eden) where they would enjoy the goodness of God. This Promised Land, also known as Canaan, was deliberately positioned at the crossroad of the known world at the time because God intended for everybody to see them as they modeled what becomes of a nation that honors God and lives under His rule. They were commanded to be show-offs. God wanted all eyes on them to bring glory to God and demonstrate His goodness on Earth.

Before Abraham became the father of the nation of Israel,

he was an older man without children. When Abraham was 100 years old, his barren wife Sarah miraculously gave birth to a promised son. They named him Isaac. Isaac had a son named Jacob (whose name gets changed to Israel), and Jacob had 12 sons who became the 12 tribes of Israel, also known as the Israelites. Those 12 tribes would be given land as their inheritance and have so many descendants that they would become a whole nation. They enjoyed God's blessing and favor on their nation as they thrived in the land God had given them for a time, but famine arose. This famine would force the Israelites to move from Canaan to Egypt, but by several divine circumstances, Jacob's son Joseph would precede the family in Egypt. And because Joseph was well-loved by the king, the family's life in Egypt would be blessed. The Israelites set up camp in Egypt, and though it was not their land, they flourished and thrived because of their covenant relationship with God. By the end of Genesis, God's promise is partially complete to Abraham to make his family line into a great nation. The Israelites, led by Joseph, have now become a thriving people in Egypt.

The book of Exodus starts detailing what happened after the death of Joseph. A new king who didn't know Joseph or his family came into power in Egypt. This king becomes threatened by the Israelites because there were so many of them, and they were so successful that the king believed that if Egypt didn't do something, the Israelites (because of God's blessing) would become so great in number and in power that they would overtake Egypt and become the new rulers. So, the

Egyptian king decided to make the Israelites slaves, and life became unbearable for them. The Israelites called out to God to deliver them from the oppression and hardship of Egypt, so God raised a leader among them by the name of Moses, who was instrumental in leading God's people out of slavery and out of Egypt. God sent Moses to usher the children of Israel to their Promised Land. First, he led them to Mount Sanai, where they established a covenant with God fortified by laws (known as the Old Covenant).

God promised to give His people back their land and make them successful if they obeyed the nearly 600 commands in the Old Testament Law. These laws are located in the books of Exodus, Leviticus, and Deuteronomy and detail the instructions for how the children of Israel were to maintain their relationship with God. Only if they adhered to these laws perfectly would they keep God's blessing. The law was given to set them apart from other nations. It provided moral principles and regulations for every aspect of their lives. The law was God's way of ensuring that they were completely different from any other group and were holy (special) to Him. That same law, however, only proved that they could never, in their human ability, fulfill every aspect of it and therefore needed a Savior to save them from their sins instead of trying to be good enough to save themselves.

Pause

You may be wondering why it's necessary for the Old Testament to focus so much attention on one nation and how this narrative has anything to do with us today. We can't afford not to understand the story of Israel because their story teaches, warns, and inspires us. Israel's story is our story—it explains how a chosen people successfully maintain a relationship with a Holy God. We pay extra close attention to the stories the Bible tells about the mistakes they made in serving God. These stories exist as warnings to teach us what not to do. And if we are to understand our place in God's plan, we must pay attention to God's plan for Israel.

Okay, back to the story.

The book of Numbers details the Israelites' journey from Mount Sinai to the plains of Moab on their way to the Promised Land. Under the leadership of Moses, the Israelites wandered in the wilderness for 40 years before they reached Canaan. Their wilderness years are characterized by God teaching them how to serve Him and chastising them when they don't. The book of Deuteronomy records the sermons Moses teaches to prepare God's people for the land they are about to possess. In the book of Joshua, they finally make it to the Promised Land under a new leader named Joshua, Moses' successor. They are gifted the land God promised to their fathers, Abraham, Isaac, and Jacob. This land, in Scripture, is pictured as a "second Eden," a good land that resembles God's original intentions for mankind.

There is only one problem.

Strangers currently occupy the special land God had set aside for His people. These strangers do not know or worship God. In fact, they worship idols and have religious rituals that diametrically oppose the worship of the one true God. So, God makes a very stern request and warning for His people: He tells them that when they get to the Promised Land, they are not to cohabitate with strangers. They are to completely drive them out of their land because if they allow them to stay, their behaviors, customs, and religion would inevitably rub off on the Israelites, and they would slowly begin turning away from their God and religion. For the Israelites, the rules were quite simple: Obedience equaled success, and disobedience meant failure. The book of Joshua ends with the children of Israel settling in the land they were promised and poised to be the picture of favor and blessing God intended.

Unfortunately, when Joshua dies, the Israelites give in to the foreign influences of the people who live among them (you know, the ones they were supposed to drive out of their Promised Land), and they start to worship their idol gods. This causes God to withdraw His protection, and their enemies eventually conquer them. The book of Judges describes the downward spiral of the children of Israel due to their inability to live up to the standards of a holy nation. But God never forgets His promise to the patriarchs; He sends the Nation of Israel several judges who act as interim leaders that lead the nation and save them from their enemies. The judges would lead the people to victory against their enemies. Then, they would repent and walk in the ways of God. But when that judge would die, the Israelites would rebel again and be overtaken by their enemies, a new judge would lead them back to repentance, and the cycle would start all over again.

Samuel was their last judge, but he was also a prophet. Before he died, the people begged him to give them a king to lead Israel because they wanted to be like every other nation run by a king. The problem was that God never intended for them to have an earthly king like every other nation. He called them to be different because God knew that their acceptance of an earthly king was their rejection of Him as their Heavenly King. But the book of first Samuel depicts how God gives them what they want, and Samuel the prophet anoints a man named Saul to be their king.

Consequently, with every earthly power comes the potential for corruption, which was the case with their new king Saul. At first, his reign leads the people to experience victory against their enemies. However, Saul's disobedience jeopardizes Israel, and God is forced to replace him with a new king who would obey God and lead the people faithfully. The beginning and end of kingship in Israel are depicted in three series of double books called I Samuel and II Samuel, I Chronicles and II Chronicles, and I Kings and II Kings. Read through the history of Israel's kings—most of them were fascinating characters. The double books are where most people become a bit overwhelmed with keeping up with the story, so here's a hint: If Chronicles seems redundant, it's because it covers much of the same ground as the books of Kings.

Enter the most famous king of Israel, King David. David is not a perfect man but faithfully rules the kingdom, and he is considered "a man after God's own heart" (1 Samuel 13:14). Initially,

Israel enjoys rest from war with their enemies and prosperity as David successfully secures their borders and ushers in a time of peace. David sets up his throne in the largest city in Israel called Jerusalem (a.k.a. Zion), which becomes a fixed place where God will dwell among His people. When David builds his palace, he also desires to build a home (temple) for the Lord where God's people could meet with Him and worship Him. But a prophet reveals to David that he is not the king through which this temple will be completed. God plans to use David's son to build the temple. Israel's prosperity does not last because David falls into sin. But because of his faithfulness to God and his repentant heart, God promises to establish David's kingdom forever and that the throne would never depart from his descendants. Jesus Christ is a descendant of David and eventually establishes a Heavenly Kingdom just like David established an earthly one, thus fulfilling the prophecy and promise that David's dynasty would last forever.

David is succeeded by his son Solomon who becomes a wise and prosperous king. He is considered the wisest man that ever lived, and most scholars credit him with authoring three of the books of wisdom: Proverbs, Ecclesiastes, and Song of Songs.

Ecclesiastes and Proverbs are full of wisdom and remain relevant today. Solomon completed the building of the temple that David endeavored to build. He built a permanent temple in Jerusalem to replace the tabernacle's temporary structure where God would temporarily dwell among His people; finally, God had an address on Earth. Solomon's time as king is summed up like this: It was a great time of fulfillment of God's promises to His chosen people. Israel had finally arrived. They were one nation, living in their own land, and the Lord dwelled among them. However, in Solomon's later years, he turned against the Lord and worshipped other gods. This idol worship ushered in an era of rebellion that forced God to withdraw His favor and protection from Israel again. The ramifications of Solomon's introduction of idolatry to the nation of Israel were dire. The kingdom was torn in two. There was now a northern kingdom (also called Israel) made up of the ten northern tribes of Israel, and a southern kingdom (called Judah), made up of the two southern tribes of Israel. Israel was led by a man named Jeroboam, and Judah was led by Solomon's son Rehoboam. These two kingdoms fought against each other, leading them to become more vulnerable to their enemies.

You may be wondering why God would allow all of this to happen. Why would a sovereign God stand by and watch as Israel's leaders perpetuate a cycle of disobedience and punishment? The answer is found in God's redemptive nature. God chose to love Israel and redeem them despite their sin and rebellion. He made a covenant with them and a promise to bless them, and they could never rebel enough to stop His plan.

The kingdom of Israel had 19 kings, and they were all wicked. And because of their wickedness, Assyria conquered them, and Israel was scattered and never again restored. This has become known as the "Lost Ten Tribes of Israel." During this episode of division and turmoil, God raised up prophets to be His voice to the nations. Throughout Israel's history, God used prophets to call His people back to Him and to proclaim the good news of the coming Messiah. The following 17 books are called the Books of Prophecy and are often divided into major and minor prophets. This distinction has nothing to do with their message or value. It is based strictly on the size of the books.

Major: Isaiah, Jeremiah, Lamentations, Ezekiel, Daniel.

Minor: Hosea, Joel, Amos, Obadiah, Jonah, Micah, Nahum, Habakkuk, Zephaniah, Haggai, Zachariah, Malachi.

The prophets brought messages of blessing and judgment as they endeavored to lead the people of Israel back to God. Still, these prophets were often hunted and killed because their messages did not agree with the rebellion Israel had become accustomed to. The kingdom of Judah had 20 kings, and only a handful was not wicked. Babylon eventually conquered them, and Nebuchadnezzar, the Babylonian king, destroyed their temple. The temple was God's symbol to Israel that they were His chosen people, and He was with them. When the temple was destroyed, so was their ability to maintain their religion, and it was a sign to Israel of God's judgment on their disobedience. The Babylonians took Judah into captivity as their slaves.

At this point, you may be tempted to think that was the end of Israel, but God never breaks a promise. He made a covenant with Abraham to bless his descendants, and He vowed to David that his house (the Davidic line) would go on forever. The Israelites may have been crushed under the weight of captivity because of their disobedience, but God always has the final say, and His plans will not fail (remember the point of the story discussed at the beginning of this chapter). Persia eventually conquered the Babylonians. Their king, Cyrus the Great, allowed the Israelites to return to their land (Jerusalem), where they rebuilt their temple and were again free to worship their God according to Old Testament Law. Although they were back in their native land, it wasn't the same. The previous lands of Judah were now called Judea, and the previous land of Israel was now called Samaria. The history of the people of Israel is found in the first 17 books of the Old Testament. Every Christian should understand the history of the nation of Israel because Israel's story is our story in Christ.

The next set of books in the Bible is referred to as the Books of Poetry:

- Job
- Psalms
- Proverbs
- Ecclesiastes
- Song of Solomon

These are also called the Books of Wisdom. The authors describe how to conform our lives to the order established by God. Through these books, we come to know true wisdom. It isn't the accumulation of facts or knowledge; wisdom is the fear of God and adherence to His way.

It's important to note that the Bible was not written in chronological order. However, some Bible translations place the Bible narrative in the order they happened. There is a 400-

year gap between the last Old Testament prophet (Malachi) and the arrival of the next prophet, John the Baptist, which marks the beginning of the New Testament. These 400 years are commonly referred to as the intertestamental or silent period because God was not directly speaking (via prophetic voice) to His people during that time. Alexander the Great conquered Persia during the intertestamental period and introduced Greek culture and language. Eventually, though, Persia was conquered by the Roman Empire, and Israel was forced to live under the brutal mastery of Imperial Rome.

New Testament

The New Testament describes the experience of the Jews/ Israelites under Roman rule. There is an emergence of differing sects of Jewish leaders, two of the most notable groups being the Pharisees and Sadducees. The Pharisees believed in radical obedience to the religious laws of Moses (i.e., circumcision, food laws, rules about the Sabbath, etc.), promoting the complete separation of Jewish people from the Pagan corruption of the Greek culture. The Sadducees were Jewish teachers of religious law but were not as concerned about separating themselves from the Romans. In fact, as recognized representatives of religious law by the Romans, they depended on the favor of the Roman Empire to maintain their influential standing in society. There were other sects of Jews (i.e., Essenes, Zealots, etc.) whose views varied between the views of these two prominent groups. The one thing most of them had in common was that they all believed God would once again deliver His people through the emergence of a king or priest who would usher in their renewed kingdom on Earth. And they believed this would happen through a violent act of divine judgment on Rome. The Jewish people knew their history and understood their covenant with God, so it's no wonder they assumed that their redemption would come in the form of God re-establishing a literal earthly kingdom in their original land. There were differing views on how God would fulfill His plan, but they believed that the Messiah whom God would send would be a mighty deliverer, not a suffering savior. And this is where a man named Jesus enters the story and completely turns the world upside down.

We can't fully understand the story of Jesus unless we understand it in the context of His story being the climax of the story of the Bible. Jesus fulfills God's original plan for humanity because through Jesus, we are reconciled, and our relationship with God is restored to its original design. Through Jesus, God accomplished His purpose for the world. Jesus' story is the story of the Kingdom of God.

Luke 4:43 makes it plain for us that Jesus was sent by the Father to do one thing: Preach the Gospel of the Kingdom. The good news of the kingdom of God is that God wants to take over the rulership of humanity, and He will once again dwell among His people. Jesus is the door through which man can be saved, and all who enter through belief in His sacrifice on the cross have the right to spend eternity with God.

Everything we read in Scripture, from Genesis to Revelations, points to Jesus Christ. He is the lamb of God who takes away the sins of the world. He is the descendant of David, and all who believe in Him are the spiritual offspring of Abraham, the father of faith. And He is the conquering King who will usher in the second coming of God's Kingdom on Earth.

The first four books of the New Testament are called the Gospels—Matthew, Mark, Luke, and John tell the story of Jesus' life, death, and resurrection but from different vantage points.

The book of Acts describes the beginning of the church and explains how Jesus' followers grew from a small group of witnesses to a movement that spread throughout the Roman Empire and the known world led by a man named Paul. The apostle Paul spread the good news about Jesus throughout the first-century Roman Empire. As he did, he established churches at the locations where he preached and became their spiritual leader. Through letters, Paul instructed these churches on how to live godly lives. These nine letters are found in Romans, I Corinthians, II Corinthians, Galatians, Ephesians, Philippians, Colossians, I Thessalonians, and II Thessalonians.

These books, along with the following four books of the Bible (I Timothy, II Timothy, Titus, Philemon), are the 13 books commonly referred to as the Pauline epistles (letters). The first set of epistles is addressed to churches, and the last four epistles are addressed to church leaders, teaching them how to govern God's people properly. The next eight books (Hebrews, James, I Peter, II Peter, I John, II John, III John, and Jude) are also letters, and they are addressed to believers in Christ living in first-century Rome. The book of Revelation is a book of prophecy written by John, and it foreshadows future events and the end of the world.

The End... And Beginning

In Noah's day, God grieved over the sinful nature and rebellion of mankind and destroyed His creation by a flood. At the end of the age, God will once again purify the Earth, but this time by fire. This purification will rid the Earth of evil, pain, death, and suffering, but this time it will last forever (II Peter 3:6-7, 10).

New Jerusalem (the holy city where the people of God who made it to Heaven live) will come down to Earth, and God's dwelling place will once again be among His people (Revelations 21:1-4). God's people do not spend eternity in Heaven. After being raptured to Heaven, we return to the new Earth and live forever with God (II Peter 3:13). The concept of time, as well as the Heavens and the Earth as we knew them, will no longer exist. We will live forever in the Holy City, where God is our King. Our sole purpose will be to live and glorify God as new beings with new bodies on a new Earth, just like God planned from the very beginning.

See, I told you. God always gets His way!

I want to highlight one word in the above sentence, and that word is "live." Many people have the misconception that eternity is boring and there will be nothing to do. While we aren't privy to

God's entire plan for eternity, I will tell you that eternity is not a time for resting; it's a time for living. But this time, you will really live. You will enjoy an existence that is exciting, invigorating, and joy-filled. Trust me, when you make it to New Jerusalem, you won't want to be anywhere but there, and the greatest joy you experience on Earth will be absolutely nothing compared to the fun you will have with God forever.

This entire summary points to one thing: The story of a King and His Kingdom.

CHAPTER SIX
Practically Speaking

I will admit that reading the Bible hasn't always come easily to me. If you're like me, you prefer other biblical books, not because the Bible isn't a priority, but because they are easier to understand. This has become a snare to many Christians' ability to value God's Word, and it's a deliberate trick by Satan to keep us from the very thing that has the answers we need for every situation. I view the Bible as God's gift to man to help them overcome sin, sorrow, and sickness. It's the cheat sheet for the tests of life. For example:

Sin test cheat code: Psalm 119:11.
Sorrow test cheat code: Jeremiah 15:16.
Sickness test cheat code: Proverbs 4:20-22.

Once I began to value God's Word, I understood it more. I then adopted a general rule of thumb for Bible reading: Don't become religious about it but do it religiously. Here's the difference: A religious person reads the Bible daily to feel good about themselves and make themselves look good to God. A person who reads the Word religiously reads the Word with consistent and conscientious regularity, and that diligence is rewarded with greater revelation.

I begin each day with Bible reading. I may not spend an hour reading Scripture every morning, but I religiously ingest the Word before allowing anything else to enter my spirit. I put the Word before social media, e-mails, and text messages. Heck, I put the Word before brushing my teeth. I am conscientious and consistent with ensuring God's Word is the first thing I set my eyes and heart on daily.

Why?

Because whatever you focus on first tends to have a significant bearing on the direction of your day.

I want to create a habit of allowing the Word to set the course for my day.

—

What this looks like for me is reading the Bible by book, reading a portion of it daily until I complete the entire book. I organize my study time around reading an entire book of the Bible at a time. Many of us have been taught to arbitrarily read a verse or a chapter a day, and the next day we may read an entirely different verse or chapter in a different book of the Bible. Reading the Bible this way is antithetical to your understanding of it. You must treat the Bible as a library of books. You wouldn't go to the library and check out three books and read one chapter in one book one day, two sentences in a new book the next day, and one in a whole new book the following day, would you? That's what we do when we read a portion of Genesis, Matthew the next day, and Hosea the following day. Reading the Bible like that will do nothing but confuse you. Suppose you want to understand what you read. In that case, you should read each book from beginning to end, and here's why: One of the quickest ways to misinterpret Scripture is to read a random verse without understanding its context, which can only be known by reading it in relation to what is conveyed in the verses before it and after it.

Let me give you an example of this. Many of us might be familiar with Philippians 4:13, which says, *"I can do all things through Christ which strengthens me."* What you may not know, however, is that that verse is talking about money. The apostle Paul says that whether he has a lot or a little, he uses God's strength to help him be content in any condition. But you wouldn't know that if you've never read the verses before and after this passage; that's why it's often taken out of context. When endeavoring to become a person who reads and understands the Bible, *how* you read is as important as *what* you read. I am not suggesting that you read the Bible in any particular order, but I am suggesting that you remember to treat the Bible as a library of books so that you adopt the habit of viewing each book as a complete work.

I don't know about you, but sometimes I have difficulty understanding what I've read in Scripture, so I always support what I read with a supplement. As I've stated, when reading Scripture, you must understand its context to grasp its meaning. Context brings meaning to a particular verse in Scripture in light of the Book's larger purpose. So, I always follow up my reading with commentary on the passages I've read to make sure I understand their true meaning. Bible commentary is written by Bible scholars who explain and interpret Scriptures verse by verse. Conveniently, all of this is done through an app on my phone because, well, it is the 21st century.

I use technology to my advantage, and it's great because you can get your hands on just about any biblical resource with the click of a button.

Interestingly,
the more I read,
the more I want
to read.

—

But let me be completely honest with you. There are moments I am not as consistent with Bible reading as I'd like. There may be periods when you are hungrier for the Word and periods when you feel as if you're reading to read. When that happens, I suggest reading anyway. Read and keep reading, asking the Holy Spirit to stir a hunger in your heart for the Word of God. The following are suggestions for helping to gain and maintain a healthy appetite for the Word.

1. Pray: As with anything else you need from God when it comes to the desire to read God's Word, ask for it if you don't have it. Beyond praying for the desire to read, ask God to help you understand what you read. Lastly, pray that God will enable you to apply the truths you learn in His Word to your life.

2. Be consistent: For Bible reading to become a regular part of your life, you should set aside a standard time to study. Set aside time daily, multiple times a week, or whenever your schedule permits. But the key is to make it a regular appointment you do not miss. My suggestion on how often to read would be the same as the Christians in Berea, who were praised by Paul for their nobility and eagerness to study the Scriptures daily.

3. Have a plan: Bible reading is easier when you approach your study time with a plan. There are a variety of Bible plans to choose from. While reading a book in the Bible, build your study around searching the Scriptures to see what else it has to say regarding the passages you are

reading. There is a practice I learned many years ago in church called "tying up your Bible," which simply means that you make ties between different passages that support each other or lend greater revelation concerning the broader meaning. For example, there are countless scriptures in the New Testament that either directly quote or reference scriptures in the Old Testament. When you tie up your Bible, you note these instances, which allows you to build a broader understanding of the text with the understanding that Scripture supports itself. Note: If you read about a particular character in the Bible, the story may be about them, but the theme is always about God. Their story has been included in Scripture because it is meant to tell us something we need to know about the character and nature of God.

4. Choose the right translation: The Bible was translated from its original languages (Old Testament – Hebrew; New Testament – Greek). In doing so, translators were tasked with making the text convey precisely what was meant by the writer in the original manuscript. This is a challenge, considering various portions of the English Bible may not convey the exact thought of the writer. Nevertheless, different Bible translations seek to make Scripture as reliably consistent with the original text and as easy to understand as possible. Translations are usually on a spectrum ranging from:

   a. Those that seek to provide word-for-word translations. This means that scripture is translated from one language to the next, with the translator being diligent in staying true to the word structure of the original text.

    b. Those that seek to provide thought-for-thought translations. This means that Scripture is translated from one language to the next, with the translator less focused on the words and more focused on conveying the thought/idea of the original text.

I like to use a translation that fits in the middle of this spectrum. I want a text as close to the author's original words and thoughts as possible. The translation that fits this description best is my favorite, the New Living Translation (NLT). The NLT seeks to be true to the original Greek and Hebrew text to preserve the meaning, but it's also extremely readable and easy to understand. Regardless of the translation you choose, the goal is to read it and understand it.

    5. Choose the right tools (three basics).

    a.   Bible dictionary: Contains definitions of keywords found in Scripture. This tool can be used to learn more about names, places, concepts, etc.

    b.   Concordance: Contains every word used in the Bible and the location where it can be found. It helps us understand how a word is used, where it is used, and how many times it is used.

c. Bible commentary: Contains an in-depth explanation of a particular passage in the Bible.

d. Bonus: Four free Bible study apps –

1. Blue Letter Bible

2. YouVersion

3. Matthew Henry Bible Commentary

4. Got Questions?

Overcoming Common Barriers to Reading the Bible

Why don't Christians read the Bible? There are, no doubt, myriad reasons, but I'll focus on three of the most common responses to this question and provide a practical solution.

1. *"I can't understand it."* Here's some good news for anyone with difficulty understanding the Bible—You are not alone. I'd venture to say that no one picks up the Bible for the first time, and everything clicks for them immediately. I spent many years reading things I didn't understand until the Holy Spirit (the Teacher and Revealer) helped me. We should not allow our limited understanding to prohibit us from picking up this Book. When we teach our children to read, they are constantly reading things they don't understand, but if we made them wait to read until they understood what they were reading, they'd likely never start reading. The same goes for Bible reading. Do not wait to understand everything you read before you make a habit of reading. The Holy Spirit, in John 16:13, is called

our Teacher and our Guide and will bring meaning and significance to what you read when you ask. In Ephesians 1:18, Paul prays for the church in Ephesus and prays for something interesting. In verse 18, he prays that the "eyes of their understanding would be enlightened." He prays that their hearts understand the promises and principles in the Word of God. Why didn't Paul pray for their minds to understand? Because he knew that an intellectual understanding of the Word would profit them nothing if it did not change their hearts. And that is why we must ask the Holy Spirit to make God's Word clear to us. But you will never reach that goal if you don't pick up your Bible and start somewhere. One of the most common reasons many people don't understand what they are reading is due to the major differences between our culture and the cultural context in which the Bible was written. Authors often write, making inferences about what they assume the reader will already know and understand about the period in which they are living. If I were writing about politics today, I'd assume you knew of the current president and vice president. I wouldn't go out of my way to explain what I think you already know. The Bible was mainly written for a Jewish audience. The writers wrote from the standpoint of Jewish culture and history. So how do we address the cultural gap issue? The key is to immerse yourself in the cultural context of the writing. Do not deal with the text superficially. Dig for a deeper knowledge of what life was like for the people of that day. If I were reading Shakespeare, I'd need to immerse myself in the culture of the English Renaissance to grasp the concepts he highlighted in his writings. Without a basic understanding of life at that time, it would be easy for me to lose interest in his writings as most of it would be over my head, so to speak. The Cultural Backgrounds Study Bible is a great resource to aid our understanding of the Bible in its original cultural context.

2. *"I don't know where to start."* I get this response a lot when I ask people if they are frequent Bible readers. First of all, all Scripture is useful (II Timothy 3:16). You should read all of it, and there are no parts more important than others. A great place to start or return if you find yourself in a season when you have lost interest in the Bible is to start where you left off, keeping in mind that your goal should be to read the Bible one entire book at a time. Until now, you may not have recognized the importance of reading the whole Bible. However, as a Christian, this entire Book, not just parts of it, should consume our lives according to Joshua 1:8. I understand it is possible to have been a Christian for years and only have read about 20% of the Bible. I'm ashamed to say that I was that Christian for many years. Reading bits and pieces of Scripture is like living in a huge mansion but only utilizing two or three of its rooms. Can you imagine packing yourself and your belongings into one room when the whole house

is yours? The whole Bible was written for your benefit. You cheat yourself when you limit your access to a small portion of it. So, if you're looking to return to the Word of God after a season of not reading, simply pick back up at the last book you completed. Remember that the Bible is a story. If you want to understand the whole story, you should read the whole book. Reading the Bible from the beginning to the end helps us answer one important question: Why was this Book written? Once we can answer that question, we are better prepared to receive greater revelation regarding the truths of the Word of God.

- Note: If you find it difficult to overcome the fact that the books of the Bible are out of the chronological order in which they were historically written, a great resource is a chronological study Bible. There are several to choose from.

3. *"I have no time."* You always have time for whatever you do first. If you never have time to read or study your Bible, try doing it before you do whatever else is on your agenda. People rarely say I never have time to brush my teeth. Why? Because we tend to do that before anything else, and because it's first, it's always done. Prioritize your time in the Word and see how quickly it begins to fit into your daily schedule.

CHAPTER SEVEN
Apologetics

This entire book is dedicated to helping you grow in the knowledge of God's Word, but that knowledge isn't just for you. I began this book with a story of how my ignorance of God's Word kept me from sharing my faith. But to be clear, the letter from my neighbor did not require me to share my faith; it necessitated my ability to defend it. The art of defending faith is what we call apologetics.

Apologetics seeks to answer many questions, but the central idea is this:

The unbeliever isn't asking *what* **they should believe but** *why.*

—

As Christians, we can't simply tell people what we believe; we must be ready to tell them why. The word apologetics comes from the Greek word *apologia*, which means defense. An apologist defends doctrine with systematic arguments. Simply put, apologetics serves three main purposes:

1. It communicates what we believe.
2. It communicates why we believe what we believe.
3. It provides substantial evidence to prove what we believe is true.

So that you know, every Christian is commanded to be an apologist. We have a basic duty to defend our faith.

"Instead, you must worship Christ as Lord of your life.
And if someone asks about your hope as a believer,
always be ready to explain it."
(I Peter 3:15)

I'd venture to say this has been the missing ingredient to effective witnessing. It's not enough to have hope. The world needs more than hope; the world needs a good reason to hope. And that's what apologetics seeks to do. It's the reasons we give for why we have hope. I want to help you become less intimidated by the notion of defending your faith. I want you to be far more equipped than I was to dispute the religious beliefs of pushy neighbors. I couldn't respond to my neighbor's challenge of my faith because my neighbor, who was not a Christian, had more conviction and knowledge of her false beliefs than I had about my true ones. I vowed never to be backed into that corner again, and I want to help you do the same. It's been said that the best religion to defend is Christianity because it's the only one that's true. Well, this chapter will help form the foundation for building the defense of your faith. I'm not a philosopher nor a theologian, so this is a 30,000-foot view of apologetics. These are just the basics, so don't stop here. Find other questions that unbelievers may have and be ready to answer.

Why Is Apologetics Intimidating?

There are several reasons a believer may be intimidated by the idea of defending their faith. First, if we were honest, we'd have to trace the intimidation back to the fact that we have been willfully ignorant concerning Scripture. Remember, I told you that the danger of being a stupid Christian is not that you don't know the Word; it's that you don't care that you don't know the Word.

The intimidation stems from the fact that many of us have sat in church pews for years and years (and years) and can't string together two coherent thoughts to objectively explain the reasons why we believe the Bible is true.

———

The church is often the best place for a lazy Christian to hide. Nobody in the church is questioning you about how much you know. There's no one to explain your hope to if you avoid people who don't think like you. Then, you're precluded from the responsibility of going through the trouble of finding the answers to the questions unbelievers have about the God you say you know but can't defend. (Yikes! I'll be nicer in a minute, I promise.) This type of Christianity is the equivalent of being on a sports team and attending all the practices but never actually playing the game. So many Christians are stuck in huddles every Sunday morning where they chant and cheer and are indoctrinated on how great the team is, but the team's skill has never been tested because they've never had to play defense against another team. All teams look good in the locker room, but it's what you do on the field that matters. It's time for Christians to get out of the huddle and onto the field.

Another reason we are intimidated by apologetics and the questioning of our faith is that we don't believe our beliefs. I attribute this to the erosion of our society's concept of absolute truth. We are obsessed with the idea of freedom, but not true freedom. Instead, it's warped freedom that says we are all free to hold whatever beliefs we want and to set our subjective benchmarks for rightness. This is done in the name of inclusion. Nobody is wrong; therefore, nobody is right either. We want to create this space where values are subjective, so we don't offend each other. This creates fluid Christianity that changes based upon the degree to which it's challenged. There is nothing subjective about truth; it is absolute.

Absolute: an unchanging point of reference by which you gauge a certain position of right and wrong.[5]

Truth: that which is in accordance with fact (the standard).[6]

If I say I have a two-inch string, that statement is only true based on the standard measurement of inches, which is fixed and unchanging. If my string equals the standard length of the measurement of two inches, then what I've said about my string being two inches is true.

Absolute truth: That which is always valid.

---

[5] "Absolute." *Merriam-Webster.com.* 2022. https://www.merriam-webster.com (1 January 2021).
[6] "Truth." *Merriam-Webster.com.* 2022. https://www.merriam-webster.com (1 January 2021).

If truth isn't absolute, then it isn't true, and when measured against an unchanging standard it will either be right or wrong.

—

This may all sound philosophical, but it's just common sense. For the believer, the answer to the question of truth is easy. The truth is anything God says because His Word is the unchanging standard by which everything must be measured.

"Make them holy by your truth; teach them your word,
which is truth."
(John 17:17)

The absolute truth for the believer is anything in line with the unchanging standard of God's Word. If you don't know the Word, you don't know the truth, and therein lies the problem. We are easily persuaded against the truth because we don't know it. The reasons for having hope are the legs upon which our table of truth stands. Without those legs, our truth has no support and can topple with the slightest pressure. If you've got shaky faith, there's only one solution—search the Scriptures for truth and the support to anchor it. We understand this isn't easy today, especially in today's society, where tolerance has replaced truth as the most important value. Tolerance is basically the idea that truth is relative (we can all be right regardless of our differing opinions) and that everyone's truth is created equal.

Furthermore, no one has the right to criticize or challenge anyone's beliefs. I'm sure you can see how this would make witnessing to unbelievers extremely difficult. If I'm not willing to tell the unbeliever that his beliefs are wrong, then I disavow my beliefs because the truth is absolute. Someone or something has to be on the losing side of that validation measurement. Jesus said I am *the* way, *the* truth, and *the* life, not one of the ways, one of the truths, or one of the lives. That sounds absolute to me.

People who don't believe in God use their unbelief to support the notion that He isn't real. For them, their truth outweighs the truth of God's Word, but there's an inherent issue with this kind of thinking. Let me give you an example. My unbelief in fat is not enough to keep me from getting fat if I don't eat right and exercise. The fact that I don't believe in fat does not negate its effects on my body. If I live as if fat does not exist, it will still affect me without my permission. It doesn't need to be validated by me to be true. The unbeliever's unbelief in God is not a strong enough argument against His existence and does not exclude them from His judgment.

The good news is that most people's arguments against the Bible can't withstand the investigation of reason. That is to say there is a reasonable answer for every objection one may encounter regarding the truth of the Word of God. Our job is to find those answers and be ready to dispense them when necessary.

Here is one word of caution before we present these defenses: Always remember that as a Christian apologist, the goal is not to win an argument but to win a soul.

———

"For we are not fighting against flesh-and-blood enemies but against evil rulers and authorities of the unseen world, against mighty powers in this dark world, and against evil spirits in the heavenly places."
(Ephesians 6:12)

What are the authorities referenced in the above Scripture? They are ideologies that exalt themselves above the knowledge of God's Word, man-made theories that sound good but can't stand up to real scrutiny. Don't ever seek to outdo an unbeliever in the presentation of a thought; seek to love them with the presentation of the Gospel. Here are my top four defenses to the most frequent questions posed by unbelievers.

Top Four Defenses

Question #1: You can't prove God is real, can you?

Answer: If I were to show you a painting, you'd have no choice but to assume that the picture did not paint itself. The painting is proof of the existence of a painter. The Earth we live on, the trees and seas on the Earth, and everything that inhabits the Earth are evidence of the Earth's creator. Attributing the existence of a planet to anything other than a planet maker would be as stupid as assuming that a painting could paint itself. The answer is common sense. However, agreeing that nothing is created without a creator isn't the same as acknowledging that that creator is God. So, let's make a case for it.

So many of us think that science and God are on two opposite ends of the spectrum in the search for truth. But you must remember that God created science. Science is the proof of God, not the objection to Him. Science is knowledge about the natural world based on facts learned through experiments and observation. The most notable scientists to whom we credit the expansion of our understanding of the world around us believed in God. Sir Isaac Newton, Francis Bacon, and Johannes Kepler were theists. Those pioneers pursued science because they believed in God, and their beliefs in the truths of science and Christianity were never at odds.

I want to give you an example of how science will lead you back to God. Two words: Intelligent design.

Sir Isaac Newton said of our solar system, "This most beautiful system of sun, planets, and comets could only proceed from the counsel and dominion of an intelligent and powerful being."[7] Intelligent design is simply identifying and acknowledging God's fingerprint on the world. Some assert that if God were real, He'd make it abundantly clear. He wouldn't be so vague about His existence to give people the opportunity to question it. But let me submit to you that He *has* made His existence abundantly clear. God has spelled out the evidence of His existence in the world. Here are two examples:

1. The cosmos

---

[7] Pearcey, Nancy R., and Charles B. Thaxton. *The Soul of Science: Christian Faith and Natural Philosophy.* Crossway Books, 1994.

2. The fine-tuning of the universe.

Let's deal with the cosmological argument first. We can reason scientifically and philosophically that anything that exists must have had a beginning. In other words, nothing exists without a cause. That painting we discussed had a beginning, a force that acted upon it because paintings don't paint themselves. Paintings don't start as paintings; they start as ideas. The painter then transfers their ideas onto a canvas. There is a date that any painter can ascribe to the origin of their creation. We can and should assume that the world we see has an origin. It didn't start as a world; it started as an idea. And if it did, whose idea was it? Just like we wouldn't attribute the creation of the painting to the painting itself, it would have had to be created by an entity greater than it. The same is true for our world. The majesty and vastness of such an intricate creation could not have been created by anything other than a powerful entity outside of it. Creations are proof of their creator.

"The heavens proclaim the glory of God. The skies display his craftsmanship."
(Psalm 19:1)

The above Scripture presents an interesting concept. It denotes that creation has a voice. How can things speak? The painting speaks to the beauty and awesomeness of the painter's mind. Our world does the same for our God.

The fine-tuning argument explains that the laws of physics

that govern the universe are perfectly suitable for sustaining human life. The slightest change to these universal principles would make our universe uninhabitable. For example, the Earth is 149,009,962 kilometers from the sun. If the Earth were just ten feet closer to the sun, the Earth would burn up. If it were ten feet further, we would freeze to death. The only explanation for fine-tuning the inner and outer workings of the world is that an intelligent mind fine-tuned it. To think that anything about our world has been left to chance is the equivalent of believing that if you put a canvas, some paintbrushes, and ten different paints in a big bag and shook it up, a beautiful painting would come. It just doesn't make sense. The world around us speaks loudly and says the same thing—it testifies to the glory, majesty, and intentionality of the God who made it.

You could attribute creation to another entity, but you'd have to work pretty hard to make it make sense.

—

Question #2: Why should I trust the Bible if man wrote it?

Answer: Have you ever heard someone say, "I don't trust the Bible because man wrote it, not God"? If you say that men wrote the Bible, you're correct and incorrect at the same time. Man was the channel through which the Bible came, but they only transcribed God's words.

"All Scripture is given by inspiration of God, and is profitable for doctrine, for reproof, for correction, for instruction in righteousness:"
(II Timothy 3:16 KJV)

In Greek, the word "given" denotes something divinely breathed. II Timothy 3:16 says that God breathed, and out came the Word. The Word that was breathed out had to have a place to land. And II Peter 1:21 says that it landed on holy men.

"Above all, you must realize that no prophecy in Scripture ever came from the prophet's own understanding or human initiative. No, those prophets were moved by the Holy Spirit, and they spoke from God."
(II Peter 1:20-21)

The Bible is 100% breathed by God and 100% written by men, but here's where most people get hung up—they say if man has anything to do with it, doesn't that also invite the propensity for error? Men are indeed fallible creatures, capable of error, but this notion shouldn't be applied to Scripture, and let me explain why. The authorship of Scripture provides a beautiful example of what comes from a unification of divine and human activity. Notice that God fully spoke, and men fully wrote. This is proven by the fact that although the Bible was written over a span of about 1,500 years and by 40 different writers who were worlds away and centuries apart, all of Scripture coherently points to one central theme: The story of a King and His Kingdom. There can be no error when the source is divine.

Further, while the Bible was given by inspiration to men, its style and delivery are not monotonous or continuous. This proves that God spoke to men, and men wrote. If God had spoken and written, it would all sound the same. But God did not overtake their bodies and put them into a trance-like state where they became transcribing robots. No, God inspired these men, who were humans with personalities and proclivities, and He trusted them as the vehicle to get His Word to the world—different vehicles, different rides. The book of Psalm does not sound like the book of Revelation because they have two different writers. But there is continuity, symmetry, and confirmation between both books because they have the same divine author.

When this statement is made, what is really in question isn't authorship but authenticity. People don't get hung up about men transcribing Scripture; they are hung up on whether the transcription was really the inspired words of God. So, let's get into it. One of the biggest problems with explaining Scripture's authenticity is that we often use Scripture to prove our point. Christians view the Bible as the final authority on all matters about life and God, but unbelievers do not have the same belief. Most world religions have their own version of a bible, and many consider their religious books to be divinely inspired. However, you wouldn't accept a Muslim's claim that the Quran is divinely inspired because it says it is; neither should you use this explanation to explain that you believe the Bible was authored by God. You need more than your own conviction to validate this claim. Let's do it this way—look at the Bible's most important claim, and if we can substantiate its validity, we can verify the validity of the Bible as a whole. The Bible's most important (and most radical) claim is found in the retelling of the life and times of Jesus Christ as the son of God. And how do we validate the existence of Christ? One word (and it's a word that piques the interest of everyone from scientists to agnostics to atheists), and that's history.

History is not easily refutable because various sources of the same account often corroborate it. To argue the Bible's authenticity, we'd have to bring up the notion that this Book has historical reliability. The one historical account that matters more than any other is the resurrection of Jesus. As Christians, we hang our entire belief in God on the resurrection of Jesus. If this were a bet, we'd push all our chips to the center of the table and risk it all because Jesus died and came back to life.

And why is this one thing so important?

Because no other religion can say the same for their messiah. Buddha, Muhammad, and Joseph Smith died and were never seen or heard from again. No matter how holy their followers claim them to be, they disqualify themselves from being put in the same god class as Jesus on that basis alone. They all have bones somewhere. Jesus is the only messiah who was born, died, and rose with eyewitness accounts to prove it. Without this distinguishing characteristic, His resurrection from the dead, there's no difference between what we believe about our God and what the Muslims or the Buddhists believe about theirs. Without the resurrection, Jesus does not earn the title He professed to carry as the son of God, and we simply cannot stand by our claims of the deity of Christ with any degree of certainty.

Paul says it this way:

"And if Christ be not raised, your faith is vain; ye are yet in your sins."
(I Corinthians 15:17 KJV)

"And if Christ has not been raised, then your faith is useless and you are still guilty of your sins."
(I Corinthians 15:17 NLT)

Most of us know that Jesus had to die but may not be aware of why He had to be raised back to life. The resurrection was the proof that He conquered one of our greatest enemies, the enemy of death. If He had not conquered death, we would not have been granted the opportunity to experience eternal life.

The various historical accounts of the person of Jesus Christ written by several eyewitnesses who corroborate the story of His life can be considered evidence of the existence of Jesus. Much like if I were to talk to the doctor that delivered you, your third-grade teacher, your best friend from high school, and your current boss, they'd all provide different but confirmatory accounts that you exist, and their connection to you would be evidence that your claim to be who you are is true. To have heard about you from these various sources, including your mother, but to turn around and deny that you existed would be pretty stupid. If you were to discover some footprints in the sand, those footprints would be proof that someone had been walking there. You'd have to attribute the existence of those footprints to some physical presence.

Jesus left His footprints all over the world, and they are undeniable proof that He was, in fact, here.

—

Paul knew this to be true. That's why he went above and beyond to point to the physical evidence of this claim that Jesus rose from the dead, which proved that He was indeed the Messiah. In I Corinthians 15, Paul tells any doubters to go and talk to over 500 people that Christ appeared to after His death. Paul basically says, "If you can't believe me, a guy who wasn't physically there, then go talk to the people who are still alive, that actually were there and did see Him in the flesh when He was supposed to have been dead."

"I passed on to you what was most important and what had also been passed on to me. Christ died for our sins, just as the Scriptures said. He was buried and raised from the dead on the third day, just as the Scriptures said. He was seen by Peter and then by the Twelve. After that, he was seen by more than 500 of his followers at one time, most of whom are still alive, though some have died. Then he was seen by James and later by all the apostles."
(I Corinthians 15:3-7)

When asked why they believe in Jesus, many people credit their faith. That's like saying, "I believe because I do." While that may be true, it isn't a compelling enough argument for me to take your claim seriously. Paul says of the resurrection that our greatest claim had to have been validated by more than faith; it needed to be validated by human experience to silence those who found it too good to be true. Let's conclude that if we can agree that Jesus was who the Scriptures claim Him to be, then we can believe the whole Bible.

"The Bible is a reliable collection of historical documents written by eyewitnesses during the lifetime of other eyewitnesses. They report to us supernatural events that took place in fulfillment of specific prophecies and claim to be divine rather than of human origin."
(Voddie Baucham)

Question #3: How can a loving God send good people to hell?
Answer: The answer to this question is short but not so sweet. The answer is that this question isn't valid because there are no good people. But for the sake of argument, let's delve deeper into this concept of goodness. Our understanding of what it means to be good is subjective. Some think that goodness is determined by what we do and will say they deserve to go to Heaven because they feed the poor, are kind to their neighbors, and try to do right by people. But the problem arises when we take a step back to ascertain the true measure of goodness. There's only one logical explanation for God's standard of human goodness, and it is comprised of a list of laws that, when kept, demonstrated righteousness. They are known as the Ten

Commandments: Do not kill, do not steal, do not look with lust, do not lie, and so forth.

One may say they don't believe in the Bible, so they don't think they need to keep the Commandments. But the problem is it's easy to dispute a person who claims to invalidate the Ten Commandments. Even people who don't believe in God have a sense of morality. Oddly enough, their morality looks a lot like the Commandments. If you ask people why they are good, even unbelievers will say things like, "I don't lie, I don't cheat, and I don't steal." And if they do, they affirm that they believe in the Ten Commandments; they're just calling it something different. They're calling it morality. Here's why unbelievers even have God's law as their standard of goodness, albeit unknowingly. Romans 2:14-15 says:

Even Gentiles, who do not have God's written law, show that they know his law when they instinctively obey it, even without having heard it. They demonstrate that God's law is written in their hearts, for their conscience and thoughts either accuse them or tell them they are doing right.

Let's take this a step further. If keeping the Commandments is the standard of goodness, we have a massive problem. There has never been a person in history who kept all the Commandments except for Jesus Christ. No one has successfully kept all the

Commandments because the Bible makes it clear that people are not born good; they're born sinful. We inherited this disease from our forefathers, who introduced sin into the world and passed it down to all their offspring. Scripture shows that sin and humanity are basically synonyms. It says:

> "For I was born a sinner—yes, from the moment my mother conceived me."
> (Psalm 51:5)
> "The Lord looks down from heaven on the entire human race; he looks to see if anyone is truly wise if anyone seeks God. But no, all have turned away; all have become corrupt. No one does good, not a single one."
> (Psalm 14:2-3)

> "And I know that nothing good lives in me, that is, in my sinful nature. I want to do what is right, but I can't."
> (Romans 7:18)

> "As the Scriptures say, "No one is righteous—not even one."
> (Romans 3:10)

No one can claim to be good because to be human is to be sinful, and sin is evil. While many people may do good things, they can't consider themselves good because, to Jesus, evil isn't the equivalent of bad deeds; it's the equivalent of a bad heart, and unfortunately, we were all born with one.

A bad heart is a catalyst for sin. Jesus said in Matthew 15:19: *"For from the heart come evil thoughts, murder, adultery, all sexual immorality, theft, lying, and slander."*

If we measure goodness based on Jesus' standard, which is the absence of sin, I've sufficiently proven that none of us are good. Thankfully, Jesus came in response to the issue of our sinful nature. Jesus took on the sin of humanity and died the death that man deserved for his sin. And because He took the penalty in our place, once we acknowledge and receive what He did, we exchange our sin for His righteousness, and His righteousness is what makes us good.

Here's something else to consider: Hell isn't the punishment for the unbeliever; the punishment is separation from God. Heaven for the believer isn't the reward. The reward is eternity with God. No doubt for the unbeliever, they have likely spent their whole lives rejecting invitations to come to God, so why would a God whom you've said no to on Earth force you to spend eternity with Him? If you reject Him down here and wind up in hell, it's because He has honored your request for autonomy. He doesn't force any of us to choose Him. Hell isn't God's choice for you; it's your choice for yourself.

For the unbeliever who spends their entire life choosing to be separate from Him, for all eternity, their wish is finally granted.

—

Question #4: If Christianity is real, why are there so many bad Christians?

As long as people are involved, the potential for misconduct and hypocrisy will exist. However, the misdeeds of a Christian does not dismantle the legitimacy of the Christian faith any more than the misconduct of a doctor would dismantle the legitimacy of the entire healthcare system. You cannot use a subjective measurement to substantiate an objective truth. The problem is in the way we view Christianity. If I take my temperature with a faulty thermometer, and instead of it reading that my temperature is 98.7, it reads that my temperature is 87.9, you wouldn't say you can't trust the standard units of measurement for heat. You'd say you can't trust that thermometer. If a Christian has moral failings, the standard of morality isn't wrong; the person is wrong.

Here's the real question: Does the hypocrisy of Christians decrease the legitimacy of the Christian faith?

Now let me tell you why that question is fair.

Christians are called to be God's witnesses on Earth. We are the instruments He uses to demonstrate His nature and be a witness of His power to the world. Rightfully so, when a Christian who is supposed to represent God falls into the same sin they claim to disagree with, it would seem as if the Gospel they are preaching couldn't possibly be true because it hasn't succeeded in changing them. We must remember that truth is absolute and isn't at the mercy of the compliance of any outside source. If something is true, it's true whether you believe it or not. And if it is false, it is false even if everyone believes it. Therefore, an accurate understanding of what we believe about our faith is critical because we don't base the merit of our faith on the degree to which followers adhere to its teachings. We base the merit of our faith on the finished work of Jesus Christ. And the last time I checked, that work was still finished.

Let this list of defenses ignite a passion in you for defending your faith. There is a world that needs answers. Friend, that answer is in your mouth. Dig deeper into Scripture so that you may be well equipped not to win an argument, but to win a soul.

CHAPTER EIGHT
What Now?

You did it!

If you're reading this, you either flipped to the back of the book to see if I fulfilled my promise to get nicer at the end, or you read it in its entirety and are now up for the challenge of turning this offensive little book into the fuel you need to kiss stupid Christianity a long, overdue goodbye. I've endeavored to increase your love for and interest in God's Word and introduce you to some foundational truths that will anchor your faith. I've also done my best to make you see that apathy in your Christian walk has catastrophic consequences for your life and the lives of the people you'll never be able to reach as long as you remain willfully ignorant of God's Word. You now understand that you are no longer allowed to say you know God if you never read your Bible. It just doesn't work like that. Hopefully, this book has prepared you to be a much more responsible Christian who understands the work that goes into living this life the right way... God's way.

So, what's next for you?

Well, that depends. I've read many books by well-meaning authors who wanted their writing to affect the reader beyond the moments they spent with the book in their hands. But there was no quantifiable way for them to determine whether the book made any real impact. What I have in common with most authors is that I'd love for what I've written to have made a lasting and profound impression on you. I'd love for you to have been provoked, enlightened (maybe a little triggered), and empowered by what you read. What I may not have in common with other authors is that I'll be able to assess the efficacy of this book immediately. I'll know these words were worth writing if it produces a wave of revival in the lives of those who read it, not a large-crowds-of-new-converts revival, but a revival of the spirit that leads to a change in the heart and behavior.

I have good news and bad news. The good news is that you are not obligated to do anything after reading this.

The bad news is that you can't unsee what you've just read.

—

God will hold you accountable for what you choose to do after being confronted with the issues in your Christian walk that need to change. I implore you to take these words to heart. Read your Bible. Pick up that life-changing book every day. Open the Scriptures, read them, meditate on them, and then do them. More importantly, look for a dark place to shine. There are people you work with, neighbors on your street, people at your gym, and so on that are in the dark, and you have been strategically placed in their path to bring the truth of God's Word to them so that the Kingdom of God can advance. You have the tools you need to do that now. Friend, I challenge you to share your faith. But don't worry; you don't need to be a Bible scholar to do so. You just need to be committed to growing in the knowledge of God.

I don't believe you read this book by coincidence. I believe you are on the verge of an exciting new journey with the Lord that will change you and those around you. If you are up for this challenge, congratulations! You are officially a smart Christian.

ACKNOWLEDGMENTS

I talked myself out of writing this book multiple times. It actually took me about three years to complete. It didn't take three years to write or research; it took three years to overcome the doubts and fears that tried to keep me from fulfilling this assignment. During those three years, multiple people spoke into my life prophetically. Many of them had no idea I was writing this book but somehow were used by God to talk my purpose off the ledge. There is always a silent support system behind every author that helps to ensure they accomplish the task at hand. I'd like to thank my support system.

To Abisola Okanlawon, Chanel Garrett, and Mirsha Alexandre: Thank you for valuing this book enough to read it first. Your honesty and encouragement have meant so much to me.

To my book squad: Laci Swann and Sharp Editorial, Justin Smith of JMSmith Branding, and Chantee The Designer & Co.- this has been a long journey. Thanks for taking this ride with me.

To the Encouragers – Nodica Browne, Chanel Garrett, Chaka

Butler, and Marcelline Girlie: You have spoken prophetically over this book, keeping me encouraged and focused on my assignment in the moments I needed it most. Chanel and Chaka, your dreams, Nodica, your words, and Marcelline, your pep talks are large parts of the reason that this book was completed. Whatever this book accomplishes in the lives of those who read it, much of that credit will go to your accounts. Thank you.

To Valerie Davis (a.k.a. "Auntie Val"): You have always been a consistent source of encouragement for me. When you called to share your dream with me, it breathed new life into this assignment at a time when I had given up. Thank you.

To my sister, LaShonine: You were my first role model. Thank you for modeling what it means to be a real Christian.

To my mom and dad: Your love, support, wisdom, and passion for God are the reasons I am who I am. I am eternally grateful that God gave me to you. Thank you.

To my children – Paige, Roman, and Jackson: Everything I do, I do for you. You three are my greatest inspiration. I pray daily that God enables me to train you to be Christians who change the world.

To my George: Honey, the words "thank you" are not adequate to express my gratitude for the love, support, correction, leadership, and strength you give me every day. It is my life's honor to be your wife. No one could be married to me but you (haha). You cover me and allow me to thrive. You challenge me and uplift me. I am everything I am because you love me.

To my best friend, my Lord and Savior: All that I am and ever hope to be, I owe it all to Thee. To God be the glory!

ABOUT ERICA BERRY

Erica Berry is a wife, mom, Bible teacher, women's ministry director, and writer with a heart to see people develop a passionate relationship with God. Her mission is to present the message of Christ in a way that challenges believers and changes unbelievers.

Having been born into a family of ministers, Erica developed a love for God and people at an early age. Her love for people led her into the field of psychology, and she now holds a master's degree in clinical mental health.

Erica's love for God led her to the ministry. She is most proud of being a third-generation Bible teacher. Erica is committed to preaching the Gospel and fulfilling her assignment to challenge the status quo of Christianity by lovingly and confrontationally calling believers to a higher standard.

Connect with Erica at www.ericaberry.org. Say hi on Instagram @_ericaberry_.